Dedication

Dedicated to those who seek to create a strategic

Contents

Strategic Planning – A Pragmatic Guide

John H. Dobbs & John F. Dobbs
Pragmatic Strategy Partners

ISBN: 9781521012192

Strategic Planning: a Pragmatic Guide

Strategic Planning:
A Pragmatic Guide

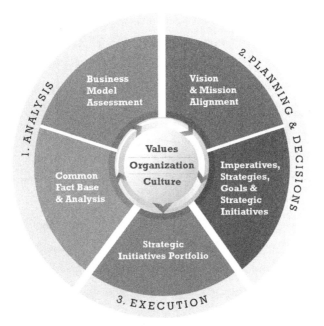

It ain't what you don't know that gets you into trouble.
It's what you know for sure that just ain't so.
– Mark Twain

When it comes to strategic planning, the saying seems doubly true. Development and deployment of sound, difference-making strategies suffer when we rely on beliefs and facts that just aren't so – including faulty analysis, gut decisions, bad assumptions, unanticipated risks, lack of decision-making criteria, and lack of agreement on direction and priorities. You have likely seen these derail seemingly brilliant strategic plans before – and they aren't uncommon topics in many texts on strategy.

If these topics are so common in strategy books and articles, why then did we write another book about strategic planning? Based on our experience with strategic planning (which we'll get to shortly), we believe that these topics require more than an academic nod, that a real-world pragmatic approach can eliminate most of these issues. In fact, we have found that seven straight-forward practices, if followed in the planning process, increase the probability of successful strategic plan development and execution.

The seven practices needed for better strategic planning are:

1. Start with a practical, pragmatic approach to planning, rather than an academic, theoretical one
2. Follow a clearly defined, sequential planning model that is decided on in advance and accepted by participants
3. Ask and answer *necessary and sufficient* questions at the right times and at each stage in the planning process
4. Use objective criteria for decision making
5. Create alignment among stakeholders around key facts, assumptions, and decisions
6. Commit to and manage a *reasonable* portfolio of strategic actions or initiatives
7. Acknowledge reality in order to foster self-honesty

This book has been designed as a practical guide to help your organization, regardless of size, magnify these practices to realize the successful creation and execution of your strategic plan.

An Approach Born of Dual Perspectives

As the authors approached the topic of strategic planning, our different backgrounds not only allowed but compelled us to approach the topic and the concepts involved from different perspectives – one from an external consulting perspective and the other from an internal management perspective.

The first perspective is one of a professional external strategy consultant who has spent many years consulting with organizations large and small on their business, internet, business process, and IT strategies. From this perspective, it's evident that the processes and methods used to develop and arrive at consensus on strategic direction are as important as the strategy itself. Also, even with a consultant involved in strategic planning, consulting advisory projects end and organizations must ultimately execute long-term strategies successfully on their own, without the consultant's ongoing participation and guidance.

The second perspective is that of an internal executive, a VP of strategy for a major corporation who is painfully aware of the many twists and turns that occur between strategy formulation and strategy implementation. He had the responsibility for not only formulating strategy but also driving it forward and making it work. This experience brings to light a couple of facts. First, this task is never a simple as you might at first believe. And second, the realities of organizational limitations like skills, capacity, innovation, resources, politics, differing opinions, finances, and so on have a great deal to do with the success of any strategic plan.

The methods and practices we describe owe much of their pragmatic value to our ability to keep these two differing perspectives continually in mind as we outline this process.

1. The Strategy Landscape & Core Issues

What's Happening with Strategic Planning?

Has the need for strategic planning changed? Has it become outmoded? Is it less important today? Is it still as valued as it has been in the past?

Little evidence supports an assertion that planning at a strategic level has become any less important today as a business priority. In fact, given the accelerating pace of change in business conditions, value shifts, and technical innovation – as well as the need to address the unrelenting speed of business model deterioration – effective strategic planning may be more important now than it has ever been.

A 2015 global *Survey of Management Tools and Trends* indicates that strategic planning remains a popular activity in businesses in the U.S. and around the world. Summarized results of the survey include this statement: "Comparing the top 10 management tools over a 10-year period, Strategic Planning, Benchmarking, Outsourcing, and Mission and Vision Statements consistently remain in the top 10."[1] When 25 different tools are positioned on a usage vs. satisfaction matrix, strategic planning ranks in the upper right (positive) quadrant of the matrix. The satisfaction level for strategic planning, however, falls below several other management techniques, such as data analytics, customer segmentation, TQM, digital transformation, and disruptive innovation. An interesting side note is that companies in Latin America more frequently use (and are more satisfied with) their strategic planning efforts than are North American businesses. As an indication that strategic planning may actually be increasing in importance, the survey reveals that there were intentions by more than 30% of the organizations surveyed to make greater use of strategic planning in 2015 when contrasted with 2014.

The *2014 Board Practices Report: Perspectives from the Boardroom*, the ninth edition of a report by the Society of Corporate Secretaries and Governance Professionals, presents findings from a July 2014 survey of the Society's membership from more than 1,200 public companies. The questions cover 16 board governance areas, including established board practices and new trends. The report finds that strategy is the first priority topic for boards in 2015, and survey results show that 52% of respondents say that strategic objectives are discussed at every board meeting. Another 29% said such objectives are discussed annually. With regard to discussion of strategic objectives, some respondents selected the "other" answer choice and gave examples such as:

- An annual "deep dive" updated during the year
- Annual topic plus discussion at other meetings
- Semi-annual topic and more frequently when needed

While the frequency of offsite strategy retreats may have decreased, strategic discussions have not. Strategic planning has been evolving based on the changing needs of today's business environment. One example is the need for more timely strategic decisions. Planning cycles have in many cases been shortened in response to technology-driven and market-driven compression of product and service lifecycles. Some companies have even adopted a more frequent so-called "evergreen" planning process. But shortened planning cycles and horizons are just one example of the changing landscape which today's strategic planners face.

A recent AT Kearny study[2] of 2,000 executives finds that:

- 62% of executives say strategy development is more difficult than a decade ago.
- 74% are spending more time on strategy development.

- 46% of respondents state that strategy fails broadly or doesn't deliver on some fronts. Even worse, many companies suffer from some form of "leadership illusion."
- 81% of C-suite executives are satisfied with their strategies, while only 52% of next-level management agree.
- 42% of survey respondents think that the root causes for strategy failure can equally be found in strategy formulation and deployment.

C-Suite Challenges

A separate study of more than 4,000 executives[3] conducted between 2010 and 2015 identified the percentage of surveyed C-suite execs who identified these tasks as "significant challenges" at their companies:

- 50% - Setting up a clear and differentiating strategy
- 50% - Communicating strategy and getting buy-in
- 56% - Allocating resources to properly support strategy
- 55% - Ensuring that day-to-day decisions align with strategy
- 53% - Quickly translating strategic decisions

Digital "Transformation" Requires Strategy

Many organizations are now challenged by technology- or digitally-driven transformation. To understand both the challenges and opportunities associated with the use of social and digital business strategies, MIT Sloan Management Review conducted its fourth annual survey of more than 4,800 business executives, managers, and analysts from organizations around the world.

The survey, conducted in the fall of 2014, captured insights from individuals in 129 countries and 27 industries. One of the key findings is that digital strategy drives digital maturity. "Only 15% of respondents from companies at the early stages of what we call digital maturity – an organization where digital has transformed processes, talent engagement, and business models – say that their organizations have a clear and coherent digital strategy."[4]

In 2017, McKinsey released results of a study designed to differentiate between the winners and losers in digital transformation efforts.

They found that more than twice as many leading companies closely tie their digital and corporate strategies than don't. What's more, winners tend to respond to digitization by changing their corporate strategies significantly. This makes intuitive sense: many digital disruptions require fundamental changes to business models. Further, 49% of leading companies are investing in digital more than their counterparts do. Compare this with the mere 5% of the laggards who invest in technology – 90% of which invest less than their counterparts. It's unclear which way the causation runs, of course, but it does appear that heavy digital investment is a differentiator.

Leading companies not only invested more, they also did so across *all* of the dimensions they studied. In other words, winners exceed laggards in both the *magnitude* and the *scope* of their digital investments. This is a critical element of success, given the different rates at which these dimensions are digitizing and their varying effect on economic performance. The research suggests that the more aggressively companies respond to the digitization of their industries – up to and including initiating digital disruption – the better the effect will be on their projected revenue and profit growth.

A key conclusion of the study: "Bold Strategies Win – In the quest for coherent responses to a digitizing world, companies must assess how far digitization has progressed along multiple dimensions in their industries (e.g. marketing; customer service; supply chain) and the impact that this evolution is having – and will have – on economic performance. And they must act on each of these dimensions with bold, tightly integrated strategies. Only then will their investments match the context in which they compete."[5]

The Internet of Things (IOT)

Lest we erroneously assume that "digital transformation" strategies apply exclusively to the marketing and customer service dimensions of a business, consider what the concept of the Internet of Things (IOT) now means. Literally billions of devices, machines, and other equipment become digitally or remotely addressable – and even controllable. This addressability of machines and equipment is a capability that is a globally unstoppable trend that will affect businesses and their competitiveness everywhere.

For example, Sany Group (not Sony), based in Changsha China, builds pump trucks that can pump cement up the world's highest skyscrapers. The company, which is the world's eighth largest machinery maker, has built four smart, robot and unmanned vehicle-enabled factories since 2012. Engineers at Sany figure out how to make better products by analyzing information fed to a nearby data center in real-time from internet-connected machines operating around the world. The company tracks 380,000 of its internet connected concrete mixers, excavators, and cranes – now including 100 billion items of engineering data. Sany says that the integration of technology has increased capacity and slashed operational costs by at least 20%. Sany now has drilling rigs in the world's northernmost construction site in Russia, pounding the Arctic seabed for natural gas.[6]

Sany is betting that this technology will enable it to build a reputation for innovation and quality, rather than for lower prices. This change in focus represents a potentially important shift in its business model, to a large extent enabled by a digital transformation.

Is Strategic Planning Becoming Democratized?

In a 2013 HBR article, Clayton Christensen suggests that even the big name strategy consulting firms are being disrupted and as a result, modifying their business models. It appears that with a veritable flood of ex-big-name consultants on the market, many clients are hiring those resources or using smaller firms for strategy work. Some firms are also releasing software and other solutions to support "DIY" strategy development. So it appears strategy consulting is indeed being democratized with more companies opting to do strategy development with internal resources or with assistance from smaller, less well-known consulting firms.

The Issues

Anyone who has attempted to develop a strategic plan for a business – or has been involved in the process thereof – knows that there is a formidable list of problems, barriers, and issues that can combine to derail the process or, even worse, turn it into a time-consuming and frustratingly meaningless exercise. We have seen both the good and the bad of strategic planning – witnessing firsthand (and at times even contributing to) well-intentioned but flawed approaches. These flawed approaches can not only hinder organizations from developing and executing effective strategic plans, but can even endanger the business.

Many of these same issues, barriers, and flawed approaches have an impact on executive attitudes about planning at a strategic level. The results of a 2007 study of almost 800 executives showed that just 45% of these executives were satisfied with the strategic planning process. Interestingly, only 23% indicated that major strategic decisions were made within the process of strategic planning. And more than 25% said their companies had plans, but lacked an execution path.[7]

What to Do about These Facts?

In light of these issues, we propose an overarching planning process framework. When followed, this process framework enables leaders and participants engaged in strategic planning activities to better understand and manage both the planning process itself – and their roles within that process. Strategic planning efforts benefit mightily when participants have an understanding of and visibility into a clear, holistic model for strategy development – coupled with the ability to participate meaningfully in each progressively consequential step in the process.

However, before we suggest this more holistic approach to strategic planning, acknowledging some of the more important barriers and impediments to success is not only instructive, but necessary. Why? Because a competent process – one with at least a reasonable chance of success – needs to address and minimize challenging, real-world planning issues in a helpful, practical way.

Our experience suggests that three core issues often combine to diminish the effectiveness of strategic planning efforts. Each of these core issues can in turn be characterized by actions (or dysfunctional behaviors) that obstruct and prevent desirable outcomes.

Core Issue 1. Executive Misalignment

Formulating Strategy in the Absence of a Well-Articulated Vision for the Future

Strategic planning is often viewed and practiced as a numerical, analytical process, but it can and should also be visionary. No matter how well you analyze the issues and opportunities facing a business, analysis alone is unlikely to create the impetus and energy necessary to drive the organization forward. Our experience has shown that you also require a shared vision of the future and direction of the business.

In some organizations, such a vision originates from a single visionary leader. In others it results from a joint effort by key executives to define the desired future state of the enterprise. Yet, regardless of the initial source of the vision, *it is vital for the executive team to be aligned around a shared vision that defines the purpose and direction of the business.* Clarity of purpose is a powerful and required condition that serves to underpin strategic decision making.

A Harvard Business Review Analytical Services Survey completed in 2016 asked executives to rank the importance vs. the difficulty of several factors affecting plan execution. On the critical factor of "Clear Understanding of the organization's Vision and Strategy," 79% rated it important, while only 41% said their organization performs well.

Question to Consider: How do you help executives articulate and adopt an inspiring shared vision for the future of their organization?

Lack of Clarity about Planning Objectives & Process

Strategic Planning means different things to different people. Some executives view it as a brainstorming-for-next-year kind of activity. Others regard it as an in-depth assessment of the organization's current performance and future needs. For some, it is merely financial budgeting for next year. Still others see it as a comprehensive exercise to plan five or more years forward. Executives often experience confusion, if not open disagreement, about planning purpose and process. Confusion sometimes arises about who will actually lead or participate in strategic decision-making and why this is so.

For strategic planning to be most successful, those who provide input or who actively participate in the process must have a common understanding of the process and its objectives. In other words, they will need answers to the following questions:

- Why are we doing strategic planning?

- What are we trying to accomplish?
- What does the process look like?
- Who is involved?
- What are the steps, beginning to end?
- What will happen at each step?
- Who is leading the process?
- What kinds of data do we need?
- What is my role, and how will I participate?
- How will strategic decisions be made?
- How long will it take?
- How will the strategic plan affect or reflect budgets?
- How will we know if our plan is working?

Irrespective of the planning approach being used, you would be wise to ensure that those involved understand what the planning approach is and how it is supposed to work. Everyone participating needs to understand what their role in the process is (or is not) and at what points or stages their inputs will be most valuable. In this pragmatic guide, we propose a high-level *strategy development framework and process*. You can use this framework at first to provide a common understanding of the big picture and later as a more detailed set of steps to enable a sequential approach to strategic planning that is both suitable and flexible enough to meet the needs of most companies. The advantage of this pragmatic framework is that it can be explained at virtually any level of the organization and at whatever level of detail is deemed appropriate.

Question to Consider: How do we agree on and then explain our approach to developing an impactful strategic plan?

Unclear Distinctions between Strategic Planning & Budgeting

People frequently misunderstand the relationship between financial commitments for strategic plans (or initiatives) and annual operating budgets. To many, the primary purpose of strategic planning is to arrive at (or even force) budget decisions. Although strategic plans and resultant key or strategic initiatives most certainly impact budgets, they are typically not the primary driver of this year's operating budget. You can more properly think of funding for strategic initiatives as strategic investments rather than budget items. Moreover, developing a strategic plan in order to force budget decisions is unlikely to result in good strategy. Though we do acknowledge, that strategic and operating financial budgets will likely overlap.

"Strategic planning and budgeting are both essential, but they aren't the same thing," say Judah, O'Keefe et. al. of Bain & Company. "Too many companies conflate strategy and budgeting in a single process that muddies the discussion and turns priorities on their head. Instead of the most ambitious strategic ideas determining where the company should invest, the organization spends an inordinate amount of time debating math and updating budget targets, resulting in only incremental improvement each year." They further state, "Separating strategic planning and budgeting can improve the quality of strategic planning dramatically – as much as 40%. Effective teams are careful to develop processes that link strategy to budgetary and operational planning. But the budget is always an outcome of strategic aspiration, not the other way around."[8]

Question to Consider: What is the relationship between strategic plan resourcing and our operating budget, and how do we differentiate between them?

Lack of Executive Alignment on Chosen Strategies

A common dilemma with strategic plan execution is the lack of executive alignment around specific elements of the plan or the key strategies driving the plan. It has been said that "a mediocre plan well executed is better than a great plan poorly executed." This simple observation may carry some truth. As a corollary observation, we suggest "a good asset or opportunity can be squandered by poor execution, but superior execution cannot salvage a poor asset or opportunity."

As important as it is to develop the organization's strategic plan, seeking (and frequently assessing) alignment among and across each of the organization's key executives with regard to the plan is just as critical. Conversely, we emphasize that each executive has a responsibility to forthrightly discuss his or her individual issues or disagreements with the plan's key elements – and do so on a timely basis. If for example, I am unable to support a particular strategy because I don't see a problem or opportunity that justifies it, I need to make my disagreement known as early as possible in the process. Lack of executive alignment is a primary cause of strategic plans becoming the proverbial "book on the shelf" rather than a committed plan of action. Open discussion of (what are too often unspoken) disagreements serve to shed light on insufficiently justified strategies and help ensure that all pertinent viewpoints are considered.

A Harvard Business Review Analytical Services Survey completed in 2016 asked executives to rank the importance vs. the difficulty of several factors affecting plan execution. On the critical factor of "Management Alignment," 84% rated it important, while only 41% said their organization performs well.

A competent strategic planning process pays as much attention to creating alignment among executives in support of key elements of the strategy as it does to defining the strategy itself. Further, periodic testing and re-assessment to confirm the degree of leader alignment (or misalignment) with the plan and essential elements at appropriate time intervals is well worth the time and effort.

Question to Consider: How do we ensure that diverse perspectives are considered while creating executive team alignment around our strategies and execution plans?

Core Issue 2. Inadequate Preparation & Readiness for Strategic Decision-Making

Lack of Understanding of Current State: Failing to Ask the Necessary & Sufficient Questions

At its core, strategic planning is about asking and answering the right questions at the right time about the firm's current state and future direction. These questions need to be asked before making the inevitably tough decisions about the future. Some basic examples of such questions include:

Current state:

- Is our business model deteriorating?
- How are we doing vs. the competition?
- How well are our existing strategies working?

Future direction:

- To what do we aspire?
- How will we get there?
- What are our biggest obstacles?

Participants commonly approach the planning process insufficiently prepared to engage in meaningful discussions about the organization's business model, competitive positioning, and so on. Of course, executives naturally tend to be more comfortable making decisions that involve their areas of responsibility or expertise rather than the bigger picture decisions. This tendency becomes especially pronounced when the planning team has gathered insufficient data and analysis to accurately assess the strengths, weaknesses, opportunities, and threats relevant to the entire enterprise.

The types of questions that need to be answered during strategy formulation are quite different at each stage in the planning process. Some are retrospective, while others focus on current conditions or a future state. Some are about the *why*, while others are about the *what, how,* and *when.*

Within this pragmatic guide, we offer a set of specific, focused questions which we believe *must be asked* to cover the bases. Additionally, it is by addressing these questions that we help assure that participants are adequately prepared to move forward to the next stage of the strategic planning process.

Question to Consider: What questions must we ask to identify and understand our most important challenges and opportunities?

Imbalance of Analysis vs. Planning

An imbalance between the analysis and planning components of a strategic planning process affects the quality of the strategic plan. Some organizations tend toward bureaucratic analysis paralysis. Analysis goes on ad-infinitum and decisions are hesitantly made. Such hesitation results in missed opportunities.

In other firms, decisions are made more precipitously, without the depth and rigor of analysis required to justify major commitments of people, resources, and money. Such a ready-fire-aim approach can also be costly – resulting in mistakes that are damaging to the health of the business.

A well-designed planning process helps strike a healthy balance between these two extremes and creates confidence that strategic issues and opportunities are thoroughly analyzed – and yet are also acted on in a timely manner.

Question to Consider: How will we know if we have done sufficient analysis to provide appropriate context for strategic decision making?

Lack of Input & Communication about the Strategic Planning Process & Needed Strategies

Organizations that have difficulty with executing their business strategies are typically not very successful at communicating these strategies – whether internally or externally. Communication failure typically begins with a failure to tap into employees, managers, and executives at all levels for their ideas and suggestions for improving the business in early stages of the planning process.

Evidence of such lack of inclusion, can sometimes be seen when consultants experience the phenomenon of the *hidden idea*. A hidden idea is typically an idea or change that:

1. Will meaningfully improve a business practice or process
2. Was suggested long ago by an employee or supplier
3. Has to-date been ignored for one reason or another by management

Through interviews and analysis the hidden idea again emerges combined with the consultant's recommendations, but this time is hailed by management as a really good idea.

For this and similar reasons, Henry Mintzberg, a professor of management at McGill University, has called the term *strategic planning* an oxymoron. He believes that real strategies are rarely made in paneled conference rooms, but are more likely to be cooked up informally and often in real time – in hallway conversations, casual working groups, or moments of quiet reflection on long airplane flights. He states, "Effective strategies can show up in the strangest places and develop through the most unexpected means. There is no one best way to make strategy."[9]

Harvard Business Review's Analytical Services Survey completed in 2016 asked executives to rank the importance vs. the difficulty of several factors affecting plan execution. On the critical factor of "Employee

Acceptance and Buy-in," 74% rated it important, while only 32% said their organization performs well.

Leaders who are good at executing business strategies are more likely to have successfully *cascaded* specifics of business strategies (and what success will look like to employees at all levels) down and across the organization to create understanding, acceptance, and commitment.

Question to Consider: What does it take to create a sufficiently broad and deep understanding of our strategies, plans, and priorities across the organization? And how do we ensure management and employees buy in to our strategic priorities and commit to their success?

Absence of Criteria-Based Decision Making on Strategic Issues

Decisions reached as strategic planning progresses sometimes evolve as a fait accompli. Critical strategies then accumulate what we call real (but often undeserved) "decision inertia." They become difficult to resist – or even to present arguments against. Such inertia can occur because the idea just seems to make sense to most people or because the CEO or some other key executive is simply enamored with the idea. The greater the decision inertia, the more courage you require to oppose the idea or decision.

One way to avoid the *fait accompli* decision inertia trap is to determine in advance what the *criteria* will be for the decisions we will make – before we make them. If we agree on *how* we will decide what the outcomes of our strategic decisions need to be, then we are less likely to make decisions based on gut instinct or purely emotional arguments. Decision criteria need to be defined, agreed on, well documented, and then made visible to all at appropriate times during strategic planning meetings.

Question to Consider: How do we develop meaningful criteria for making strategic decisions more objectively?

Setting Unsupported Arbitrary, Premature, or Audacious Goals

Of all the decisions that an executive team can make, creating and setting strategic goals may be the most critical to get right.

We are aware of a new CEO who declared, "we will double the number of new outlets we open next year and increase our operating margins at the same time." A bold goal. While there is nothing wrong with wanting to do both of these things simultaneously, as it turns out, these goals were not realistic or achievable for the company at that time. The CEO had committed the company to major objectives that were almost certain to fail and result in a strategic blunder.

Strategic blunders can be defined as, "Making false presumptions about one's own competence or the likely causal linkages between one's strategy and one's goals." The truth is that the new CEO was not competent or well enough informed to make the goal decisions he made. While trying to impress the board with bold action, the capricious decisions he made ultimately damaged both the performance and the morale of his organization. His presumptions and assumptions about resource availability and the velocity of change his organization was capable of proved incorrect, and thus, his strategic goals were never really achievable. Others in the organization were aware of this error in judgement but were powerless to challenge. They became demoralized, and a self-defeating attitude set in. The issue can be traced to the CEO's failure to answer a few simple questions while forming his company's goals:

- What conditions must exist in the marketplace and in our organization for our goals to be achieved?
- What is the probability of our goals being achieved? Or being missed?
- What data and criteria have been used to define our goals?

- Are our goals simply "wishes" or are they objective targets?
- Do our resources and opportunities match our goals?
- Do we agree on our goals?

The BHAG concept (Big Hairy Audacious Goal) has been used by many business and government leaders to inspire and create energy for change. The goal stated by then President John Kennedy – "our nation should commit itself to achieving the goal, before this decade is out, of landing a man on the moon and returning him safely to the earth" – is one of the more prominently remembered examples. A more current example is car maker Volvo's goal that "By 2020 no one should be killed or seriously injured in a new Volvo." Both of these examples suggest that BHAGs are perhaps best suited to longer term, more visionary goals than shorter term operational ones. (In both examples, it should be pointed out, there were few downside consequences to not achieving such inspiring goals. In contrast, when a CEO tells the market they will double output without providing a detailed plan for doing so, the CEO may lose credibility, elicit skepticism, or raise concern that resources are being squandered in the process.)

When leaders feel the need to set audacious goals without concomitantly conceptualizing a workable plan, they may be doing so with slim assurance of achievability – increasing business risk and negatively impacting their own credibility. When coming into a new company or senior role, more effective executives will take some time to survey the situation and challenges they face, meet with key people, perform a fair bit of analysis, and put a plan together before committing to major changes or goals. A new CEO at JC Penney Co did significant damage to his company with an ill-considered decision to do away with periodic sales in favor of everyday same prices, a major policy shift that later had to be reversed.

Question to Consider: How should we go about setting strategic objectives goals and targets that are motivating, yet realistic and achievable?

Core Issue 3. Poor Execution & Deployment

Failure to Make Strategies "Actionable"

Linking strategies to specific actions is a major challenge (read: frustration) for many if not most CEOs. Strategists share this same concern. With 350 chief strategists representing 25 industries responding, one survey concluded that 40% of those surveyed had concerns about progressing strategies to action.[10]

First and foremost, an immediate impediment to successful strategy execution originates in fundamental flaws with the strategy itself. These flaws can arise for any number of reasons, but ultimately originate from a strategy developed with insufficient analysis or detail to:

1. Support its market premise or value proposition
2. Illustrate its sustainability (repeatability) via an understandable set of available opportunities
3. Foretell value creation via predictable revenue streams
4. Articulate the mechanisms for execution

If any one of these areas is underdeveloped, a major flaw is not only possible but likely.

Is it not inherently nonsensical to deliver a well-executed, but flawed strategy? This simply means that the strategy development process itself was poorly executed. It is likewise nonsensical to claim an excellent strategy was poorly executed. This simply means the strategy was not sufficiently examined to be sure it was feasible, given available resources. We will address these issues in greater detail in subsequent chapters. For now, we suggest that the probability of a major flaw is greater when strategy is developed by a single individual with enough power in the organization to essentially avoid justifying the proposed plan with data and analysis.

A major challenge for strategic planners and business leaders alike is the ability to translate vision and strategic intent into the actions that must occur in order to execute the strategy. This process of translation is typically called strategy *deployment* or *execution.* Deployment and execution failures are many; however, a common root cause goes back to misalignment on elements of the strategy among the same key executives who were involved in crafting, approving, or supporting the strategy. Failure to spot the symptoms of misalignment early on foretells execution problems later on.

Other reasons for failure to execute include lack of resources, lack of capability, lack of focus, inadequate prioritization, poor leadership, internal politics, poor communication, inadequate financing, incompatible initiatives, too many competing strategic initiatives or other projects, unexpected business crises, and so on.

Questions to Consider: How do we confirm that the strategies we adopt are properly supported both by analysis and by key function leaders? What can we do to ensure strategic priorities are promptly and successfully acted upon?

Pursuing Too Many Strategic Initiatives

According to a *Wall Street Journal* article, "C-suite executives often find themselves responding to a large number of 'strategic' initiatives, many of which are strategic in name only. Sandy Ogg, a former Unilever executive, says that during his eight years at the global food company, key executives could be asked to take part in more than 100 corporate initiatives at any one given moment, ranging from IT to diversity to corporate social responsibility."[11] Our experience has shown that most organizations cannot manage or execute on an unwieldy number of strategic initiatives.

Question to Consider: How do we prioritize to arrive at the right number of actionable strategies for our organization?

Summing Up

Few strategic plans completely avoid the issues discussed in this chapter. The core issues we have identified here affect strategic planning efforts at different times and stages in the process, as well as over the years in subsequent planning cycles. These issues, however, can be anticipated and are most successfully addressed when dealt with as early as possible in the planning cycle.

Moving forward, we will introduce an approach to strategic planning which we believe addresses these core issues. We call this approach the Pragmatic Strategic Planning Model. It offers a reasonably systematic, yet flexible process which will help anticipate and minimize unwanted effects of the core issues we have described. We begin with an overview of this *pragmatic* process, including its components and its fundamentally sequential logic. In later chapters, we examine each component of the planning model in greater detail. In all cases we will emphasize practical guidance for applying the pragmatic planning model.

Chapter 1 - Core Issues
Key Thoughts & Takeaways

Before proceeding to the next chapter, please take a few minutes to think about the following with your organization in mind:

What are my key takeaways from this chapter?

What issues have I observed in my company or organization?

What are the implications for my organization?

2. A "Pragmatic" Model for Strategic Planning

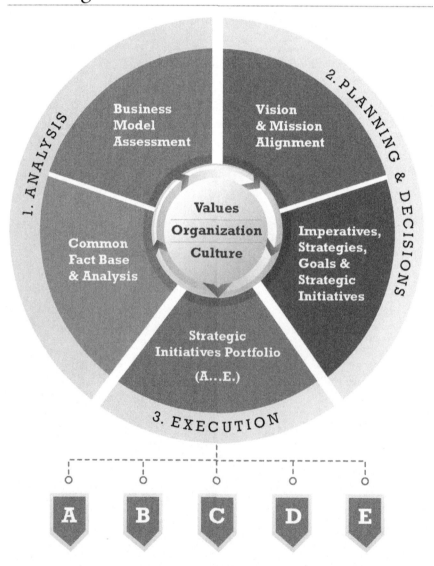

Over the years, management professors, gurus, consultants, writers, and others have put forth various theories, approaches, and analytical methods and models that can be used to enable or support strategic planning. These models encompass a variety of recommended approaches for analyzing the industry, market, products, competitive set, or conditions in which a business operates. Among the more well-known are:

- Five Forces (Michael Porter)
- Growth Share Matrix (BCG)
- Innovator's Dilemma (Clayton Christensen)
- Strategic Intent – (Hamel & Prahalad)
- Blue Ocean (Capgemini)
- Three Horizons of Growth (McKinsey)
- Strategy Styles (BCG)
- Four Levels of Uncertainty (McKinsey)
- Consolidation-Endgame Curve (AT Kearney)
- Political, Economic, Social, Technology Analysis (PEST)
- Marketing Mix Analysis (Product; Price; Promotion; Placement; People; Process; Physical – 4 P's or 7 P's)
- Product Lifecycle Analysis

Our purpose is not to recommend for or against any of these approaches, which have found broad acceptance and use in many organizations. Each is useful and valuable in its own right and under the proper circumstances. At the same time, we do suggest that none of these models provides or represents a complete, beginning-to-end analysis, strategic planning, and execution model.

The Alternative - A Pragmatic Planning Model

The Pragmatic Strategy Planning model we propose provides beginning-to-end guidance about how to more successfully manage a strategic planning process, given the complexities and real-life barriers that typically stand in the way. We propose to describe how to successfully define and deploy strategy, rather than which analytical models to adopt. In fact for simplicity's sake in this guide, we use SWOT analysis as an adequate method for assessing strengths, weaknesses, opportunities, and threats – and as a potentially useful analytical framework for a pragmatic planning process. We also use what we call a "Balanced Business Model" concept to help you determine the predicted strength over time of a company's business strategy.

The pragmatic strategic planning process comprises five major phases or stages. During each of the five stages, you can pose a series of relevant, and often critical, questions to executives participating in the strategy planning process. The ability of the management team to answer (or at least attempt to answer) these questions, to a large extent, signals the team's readiness to complete the current planning stage and move forward to the next.

For each of the five major planning stages, we offer a different set of questions for executives to discuss and answer as they participate in planning for their own organization. In addition to these questions, we also suggest actions to take (or avoid) during each stage. At the end of each chapter, we also ask you to consider implications for your organization regarding the principles and techniques in the pragmatic planning process.

Why the *Pragmatic* Strategic Planning Model & Process?

Any one of several approaches to strategy development might be appropriate for an organization. Experience tells us that the sophistication or industry focus of any given approach to strategy development may not have a great deal to do with the ultimate success of the strategic plan. Rather, the ability of the organization to align itself around and accomplish a *complete* planning process and then successfully deploy the plan are in the end what makes the difference.

An effective strategy planning process can be a powerful tool for aligning an executive team. On the other hand, an ineffective process has the potential to fragment senior executives, sow seeds of discontent, and even create active resistance among the very executives whose personal support and involvement are so critical to successfully achieve the plan's objectives. In other words, to achieve broad organizational support, the journey's path is as important as the destination. This is also important to understand: some personality types naturally tend to take an ends-justify-the-means approach, but if at least some of the ends we seek are a shared vision and unity among executive management, the *way* we get there is also critical. If you tend to focus on the results only, realize also that an inclusive approach may be the only way to achieve the high degree of alignment you seek. To create a unified team you either reach alignment on strategy and direction or else continuously replace team members. The only alternative to an inclusive approach is a fire-and-replace approach, which is not sustainable in the long run – repeated too many times, the organization becomes individualistic and chaotic.

The strategic planning process we describe here is based on many years of experience watching executives struggle with their roles in strategic planning and, even more importantly, their confidence in actually deploying the plans they have created. The pragmatic planning model we introduce here can be reasonably described as:

- Sequential
- Logical
- Thorough
- Involving and aligning for participants
- Practical

- Confidence-building

Because of the combination of the above characteristics, the Pragmatic Approach to Strategic Planning can increase the probability that:

- The organization can agree on a planning process.
- The process seems doable and practical to those involved.
- The process is simple and straight-forward, yet thorough.
- Executives are more disciplined in planning and decision making – not so likely to jump to conclusions that are premature.
- Executives become better aligned around the organization's strategy and key initiatives.
- Executives more willingly invest the time necessary to create and agree on an effective plan.
- Executives have increased confidence in successful plan execution and deployment.
- Quality of executive decisions and action plans improve.
- Strategic decisions and actions reflect organizational values and culture.

The pragmatic planning model is essentially sequential in terms of the required planning activities. Each of the five major elements of the model deserves enough time and effort in order to arrive at a plan sufficiently powerful and workable to be supported and acted on. Each element or step in the model is essential. Even if, for example, the organization has previously defined its vision or mission, current state data and business model analysis may well reveal the need to revisit that vision. Even if the need for a change in vision or mission is not obvious, guarding against unintended deviation from your intended direction is nevertheless important to review.

The Pragmatic Planning Model as illustrated in the graphic displayed at the beginning of Chapter 2 is also more likely to succeed when each of its elements has been addressed *and documented* thoroughly and thoughtfully.

A Model for Logical Sequencing of Strategic Planning Activities

To be effective and rewarding, strategic planning requires a systematic approach, supported by competent and thorough analysis. The approach should be characterized by discipline and inclusiveness. Further, the probability of successful planning greatly increases when all key players in the process work from what we call a *common fact base*. The Pragmatic Planning Model is designed to create these conditions.

The pragmatic model is simple, perhaps deceptively so. It contains three fundamental activity categories that in turn encompass five distinct planning stages and their resulting outputs:

1. Analysis of facts
   a. "Common fact base" development and analysis
   b. Business model assessment
2. Planning and decision making
   a. Vision and mission articulation
   b. Strategic imperatives, goals, and initiatives formation
3. Strategic initiative execution
   a. Initiatives prioritization and portfolio management

Planning in Context

The pragmatic model also considers a limited set of critical organizational or business contexts within which planning takes place. It acknowledges that these contextual elements already exist, that they influence strategic planning, and that they may need to be documented, formally defined, or re-defined. The three contexts are as follows.

Organizational Environment Contexts

- Values
- Culture
- Organization Structure

Each of the three primary strategic planning activity categories that constitute the pragmatic planning model – and the organizational contexts within which they occur – will be discussed at length in later chapters.

Leading a Strategic Planning Effort

To emphasize importance and increase active participation, a respected senior executive should be designated to sponsor or drive the planning process. The sponsor role assures that the planning activities actually take place, that executives and their staffs fully participate, and that the prescribed process itself is followed, at least to a reasonable degree.

Most large organizations find it necessary to have a trained professional internal planner or even an outside consultant help facilitate the planning process and key meetings. A primary role of the facilitator is to assure that all relevant opinions and ideas are both heard and considered. The facilitator also assures that thorough, systematic documentation of planning meeting or discussion outcomes and decisions occurs. Losing critical aspects of the plan over time is amazingly easy, especially the *key assumptions, data, and decisions* upon which various aspects of the plan are based. And don't forget the value you will gain from documenting that decisions were, in fact, made. A really common planning misstep is failure to document all decisions and the primary assumptions upon which those decisions are dependent.

Virtually all forward-looking plans are based, at least to some degree, on assumptions about future events, trends, and conditions. These assumptions, if wrong, obviously can lead to sub-optimization or even outright failure of key strategies and initiatives. This is critical: that assumptions upon which decisions and plans are made are agreed upon and documented. Doing so helps assure objectivity in subsequent *post-mortem* examinations of what went well and what went poorly. All too often, assumptions or decisions being questioned just before or just after delivery of a documented plan will lead to confusion or even unintended actions being taken. In most cases, the confusion may have been avoided by explicitly documenting the decisions and outcomes of the various meetings and sending out summaries to all participants at the conclusion of each key meeting. This helps assure that everyone was really on the same page as decisions were made.

Values, Culture, & Structure Play a Role

Later, we address the vital topics of the organization's culture, values, and structure. While these topics are not among the five primary stages in the Pragmatic Planning process, strategic planning is always done in the context and under the influence of the organization's values, culture, and structure. Naturally, the plan inevitably reflects these. In some organizations, values and culture need to be addressed or perhaps even re-defined to put a strategic plan in place that is authentic from a values and culture perspective.

Chapter 2 – A "Pragmatic" Model
Key Thoughts & Takeaways

Before proceeding to the next chapter, please take a few minutes to think about the following with your organization in mind:

What are my key takeaways from this chapter?

What issues have I observed in my company or organization?

What are the implications for my organization?

3. Common Fact Base Development & Analysis

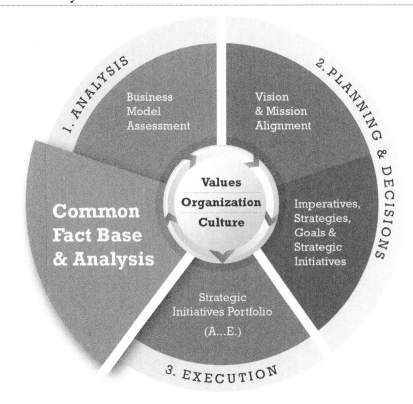

Strategic planning without good analysis is like an automobile without an engine. A primary purpose of data gathering and analyses during the initial phase of a strategic planning process is to create a *common fact base* among and across the executives involved in the strategic planning process. Why?

The process of aligning the executive team around the strategic goals, imperatives, and action plans begins by creating an acceptable level of confidence that we are making strategic decisions based on a shared, mutually agreed on set of data and assumptions. Failing to do so creates many unintended consequences as the strategic planning effort progresses. It is remarkable how easily we forget or misconstrue the conditions or data that drove decisions made even a few weeks or months ago.

The Vital Importance of a Common Fact Base

Daniel Patrick Moynihan once said, "You are entitled to your own opinion, but you are not entitled to your own facts." Such a statement could just as well be made during a typical strategic planning meeting. Executives all too frequently arrive at strategy discussions prepared with their own opinions about current conditions, preferred actions, and a set of favorite facts to support the same. We experience this as a rather common occurrence, one that may be at the root of many strategic errors committed by businesses.

Instead, a process of developing, documenting, and agreeing on a commonly accepted set of information and facts should emerge as a most desirable outcome of the analytical process. The objective of the common fact base is to ground ourselves and the rest of the cross-functional management team in the realities suggested by the relevant, available data. If thoughtfully considered, any single piece of data or analysis by itself provides one or more insights. As one set of data or analysis and its accompanying insights are brought together with another set of data or analysis and resulting insights, patterns emerge that help us identify both issues and their primary implications.

We call the most important core issues – those actually requiring decisive action – *imperatives*. When you can assemble a critical mass of facts, data, analysis, insights, issues, implications, and imperatives in a presentable form which tells a story, you then have the necessary elements of a common fact base. At this point, company leadership should gather together to become familiar with this information and consider the story that emerges.

After leadership can collectively hear the story, they are more ready to begin asking one another important questions and debate the core issues. Perhaps there is a voice suggesting that important data, considerations, or analysis are missing. Another voice might have come to a somewhat different interpretation of the facts. Encourage these expressions and discussions. If you do not provide a forum to express opposing voices or to encourage debate, you would be naïve to think that these opposing voices will not be heard in some other way. One way or another – via back channels – disagreements and other opinions will be expressed and circulated. If opinions and disagreement can only be safely expressed in private hallway discussions, then silent opposition or doubt will almost unfailingly prevent a management team from being united around a shared vision and plan.

A shared vision and plan is much more likely to emerge from a shared or common fact base, and can likewise only exist if leadership has been given the opportunity to voice concerns and come to common conclusions because of a compelling story supported by facts. If the facts are agreed and the conclusions agreed, then the imperatives become clear, and you are on your way toward a united management team committed to executing on a shared vision.

A Solid Fact Base Relies on Evidence

The concept of a strategically significant common fact base is akin in many ways to a parallel concept called "evidence-based management." In a 2006 HBR article, Jeffrey Pfeffer and Robert Sutton position evidenced-based management as a way to replace the conventional wisdom and half-truths often relied on by executives with better tested facts and arguments.

Their mantra is "Demand Evidence." This is a not new, but nevertheless valuable, expectation when it comes to developing rationale for strategic actions and decisions. During the 1980's, one of this book's authors conducted many TQM quality workshops where this phrase was not uncommonly heard, "In God we trust – everyone else, bring data!"

According to Pfeffer and Sutton, "Managers are like physicians who face one decision after another: They can't possibly make the right choice every time. Hippocrates, the famous Greek who wrote the physicians' oath, described this plight well: 'Life is short, the art long, opportunity fleeting, experiment treacherous, judgment difficult.' It's also crucial to appreciate that evidence-based management, like evidence-based medicine, entails a distinct mind-set that clashes with the way many managers and companies operate. It features a willingness to put aside belief and conventional wisdom – the dangerous half-truths that many embrace – and replace these with an unrelenting commitment to gather the necessary facts to make more informed and intelligent decisions."

To effectuate more evidentiary thinking they advocate:

1. "Asking for evidence of efficacy every time a (significant) change is proposed"
2. "Parsing the logic behind evidence"
3. "Encouraging trial programs, pilot studies, and experimentation – and rewarding learning from these activities, even when something new fails"

"Leaders who are committed to practicing evidence-based management need to brace themselves for a nasty side effect: When it is done right, it will undermine their power and prestige, which may prove unsettling to those who enjoy wielding influence. A former Netscape employee recalled a sentiment he'd once heard from James Barksdale when he was CEO: 'If the decision is going to be made by the facts, then everyone's facts, as long as they are relevant, are equal. If the decision is going to be made on the basis of people's opinions, then mine count for a lot more.' This anecdote illustrates that facts and evidence are great levelers of hierarchy. Evidence-based practice changes power dynamics, replacing formal authority, reputation, and intuition with data."[1]

So what is necessary to encourage and institutionalize concepts like evidence-based management, intellectual honesty, and common fact base development? We believe that making them a fundamental cultural underpinning and starting point for strategic planning will help a great deal, in both the short and long-term. In the section that follows we explore the use of SWOT analysis to help accomplish this.

Developing a Common Fact Base

For purposes of Common Fact Base development, a modified SWOT Analysis approach often works well. It provides a practical method for summarizing the conditions and opportunities facing a business. Objective, accurate articulation of Strengths, Weaknesses, Opportunities, and Threats can be an efficient and straight-forward way to analyze and summarize the conditions in which the business is and will be operating. The SWOT approach also lends itself to a division of labor with which to address and organize the primary categories of data needed to proceed to subsequent decision and planning stages of the model.

In order to be sufficiently comprehensive, the areas of exploration for focusing and developing the SWOT analysis should minimally include both internal and external elements:

- Internal factors
  - Products and services
  - Core processes
  - Core competencies

- o Technologies
- o People and skills
- o Financial position and limitations
- o Leadership, culture, and morale
- o R&D
- o Factors unique to your company
- External factors
  - o Customer trends
  - o Economic trends
  - o Competitors and market share
  - o Market trends and disruptions
  - o Financial and equity markets
  - o Partners and supply chain
  - o Technology
  - o Government regulations and legislation
  - o Factors unique to your industry

This list of internal and external factors is only illustrative and far from exhaustive. We offer it as a starting point for possible factors to consider in the analysis. Later in this chapter, we include a more complete set of questions to consider in initiating a SWOT analysis.

Although gathering and documenting comprehensive SWOT data is important and necessary, it is also not by any means sufficient. Answers to the various SWOT questions themselves can be compelling, but the questions then become, "What does this information really mean for us? What does our analysis suggest? What are our primary conclusions? What are the major implications of the data for our direction and future?"

Developing a common fact base that creates strategic value requires further examination of these same SWOT facts in this manner:

- **Facts:** What are the relevant, most significant, and revealing data or facts we have uncovered? What does further interpretation and analysis of these facts tell us?

  - **Implications:** What do we believe and agree are the major implications of these facts and analysis for our business?

    - **Imperatives:** What insights or preponderance of evidence emerge from the analyzed facts (and their implications) that should or must compel us to action?

By completing these additional steps beyond fact or data gathering, we signal readiness to move forward to the strategy decision and development stages of the pragmatic model. You can only move forward to the next phase when the planning team has achieved an acceptable degree of agreement and alignment around these conclusions. In a later chapter, we go into greater depth about the process of deriving strategies from facts, implications, and imperatives.

Questions to consider during Common Fact Base SWOT Analysis

*Important to our *Competitor View* Analysis

**Important to our *Market View* Analysis

What are our Strengths?

1. What are the relative strengths of our business?
2. What are our best or most unique strengths – the ones we can most profitably exploit?
3. What is our competitive or market share position? **
4. Where do we compete best? *
5. Where do we enjoy our best market share? Why? **
6. Where do we have a technical advantage? **
7. Which of our technologies is superior?
8. Where do we enjoy a financial advantage?
9. How much pricing power do we have? **
10. What are our strongest areas organizationally?
11. What or where are our best assets?
12. Which partner relationships are strongest?
13. What data or objective analysis do we have to support our *strengths* assessments and conclusions?
14. Which of our strengths are deteriorating or eroding? Do we have current data to verify or validate our strengths?

What are our Weaknesses?

1. Where do we not match up well with our competition? *
2. Which areas of our business are struggling?
3. Which competitors do we most fear? Why? *
4. Which competitors do we most admire? Why? *
5. Where do we compete least successfully? Why? *

6. Which products or services are our weakest? Why?
7. What are our financial constraints? How will they impact us?
8. Which of our financial ratios are headed in the wrong direction?
9. Where are we most unable to defend our market share? Why? **
10. Which areas organizationally are our weakest?
11. Which products or locations are affecting our results negatively? **
12. What or where are our weakest assets?
13. Which of our partner relationships are weakest? **
14. Do we have the necessary capabilities to successfully execute our chosen strategies?
15. What strengths, assets, or capabilities do our competitors possess that we lack? *
16. Are there areas where we are not competitive and should disinvest? **
17. What data or objective analysis do we have to support our *weakness* assessments and conclusions?
18. Which of our competitors is perceived by customers as creating the most value for dollars spent? *

What are our Opportunities?

1. What disruptive trends do we see on the horizon?
2. Where do we see our best opportunities to expand? **
3. Where are our best opportunities to build market share? **
4. How can we create or deliver greater value to our customers?
5. Which of our competitors is weakening? *
6. Which emerging parts of our business are most promising? Why?
7. Which adjacencies exist close to our existing business model that we could potentially expand into? What capabilities do we have that could make us successful in these adjacent markets? **
8. Whom do we view as a potential takeover target?

9. With whom could we partner or create alliances to improve or expand our business or to strengthen our business model? **

10. Where could we use technology to our advantage?

11. Whose technologies could we integrate into our products or services?

12. Where are our best opportunities to reduce costs or increase profits?

13. Where can we improve or streamline our organizational structure?

14. What are our most important R&D projects?

15. Where can we *seed* our products or technologies to gain visibility with early adopters? **

16. What adjacencies are there to our markets or capabilities that we could take advantage of? **

17. Which of our markets are growing fastest in absolute terms (size of the pie)? **

18. In which of our markets are we growing our share fastest (our slice of the pie)? **

19. What profitability or cost differences do we see in our customer segments? **

20. What data or objective analysis do we have to support our *opportunities* assessments and conclusions?

21. What are the opportunities to begin "cannibalizing" our own business (before someone else does)? **

What Threats do we face?

1. Which of our competitors (existing or new) is gaining customers at our expense? Why? *

2. Which existing or future government policies are a threat to our business or future profits? **

3. Where are we at a disadvantage financially?

4. Who might potentially view us as a takeover target?

5. Who is entering our market? *

6. Who is taking market share from us? *
7. Which of our products or services is losing market share? Why? **
8. Who is taking market share from our competitors? **
9. Who outside of our industry could be a threat? **
10. Whose business model appears to be superior to ours? Why do we think so? *
11. Which emerging technologies could threaten, disrupt, or render obsolete our business?
12. Which of our key performance or financial metrics are we most concerned about?
13. What data or objective analysis do we have to support our *threats* assessments and conclusions?
14. Which of our competitors is gaining ground or overtaking us? *
15. Where are we seeing share price erosion?
16. Where are we at risk of losing cost competitiveness?
17. How long is what we are now doing going to work?

SWOT Analysis Reveals Strategy Issues and Candidates

While SWOT analysis is a useful method for gathering, organizing, and assessing facts, it does not in and of itself result in decisions on strategy. Rather, it helps to put facts and data in perspective alongside other relevant issues and opportunities. It also exposes the trade-offs that often confront executives. For example, if a firm has both a market share gap that is unfavorable and also an unfavorable profitability level relative to competitors, we have probably identified a need to take action, but there may be important tradeoffs to consider before allocating resources. Which problem is more threatening? Which is more solvable? Which will make the biggest difference to our business? One purpose of this book is to suggest a stepped process for deciding on strategies and initiatives in a highly logical manner that encourages well thought-out, fact-based decisions.

Quantifying & Summarizing SWOT Analysis Findings

You should, of course, quantify answers to SWOT questions wherever possible. You can more effectively consider facts arising from SWOT analysis when the data is nicely organized and summarized for those who will need to consume it. To accomplish this, summarize key SWOT findings in a table like the example shown below. This helps consumers of the information better visualize and put current conditions and challenges into context. The table can also serve as a starting point for preliminary thoughts about possible future-state outcomes in areas where you require change.

Topic or Question	3 Year Historical Data	Most Recent Data	Serious Issue or Gap Exists?	Possible Future Objective or Range?
Market Share?	17%; 16%; 16%:	16.5%	Yes	17% - 18.5%
Market Share Position?	#3; #3; #3	#3	No	#2
Best Known for:?	Low Price	Low Price	Yes	Price & Value Leader
Profitability / Gross Margin?	6.2%; 6.0%; 5.8%	5.8%	No	6.4 – 6.5%
Weakening Financial Ratios?	Sales per Employee declining	$355 K	Yes	$390-$400 K
New Competitors	1	2	Yes	Defensive or Offensive Strategy?
Technology Leadership	Follower	Follower	Yes	Need to be no less than on par with the industry
Share Value			Yes – (two years out)	

The "Serious Issue or Gap" column in the above example summary can help you identify those areas where a gap exists between the organization's current performance and where it should or must be going forward. More than other areas, these areas need deeper analysis and possible scenario development as candidate targets for strategic action or initiatives as part of your strategic plan. Having identified and agreed on these *gap* issues, you can set priorities and begin to drill down on the *whys* behind them.

In addition to documenting and summarizing the SWOT factors shown above, now is a good time to consider various risks that can impact the development and execution of a strategic plan.

Testing for Strategy:
Do We Have a Viable Existing Strategy & Plan?

In addition to gathering business conditions and challenges data through a SWOT analysis approach, creating a common fact base for the executive team serves another purpose. Through it, you can assess executive knowledge and attitudes about the existing (or most recent) strategic goals plans and initiatives. Allowing executives to express their views and attitudes about *current* strategic plans and results will be extremely valuable. As a relatively simple way to assess these views about strategic planning in your organization, we offer four straight-forward questions to consider – or perhaps pose to the organization's leaders:

Question 1: What is our strategic plan?

Does our strategic plan include:

- Clearly explainable and succinct statements of strategy?
- Broad understanding of strategy by both internal and external audiences?
- Identified tangible strategic opportunities, goals, and actions?
- Progress being made against the organization's primary goals and challenges?

Question 2: Are our strategic plans working?

Is there evidence of a *viable* strategic plan?

- Articulated view of the future exists, supported by appropriate analysis, including future scenarios that illustrate value creation in the context of:
  - o Market conditions
  - o Competitive landscape
  - o Potential or existing disruptions
  - o Other uncertainties
- Strategic plan includes tangible actions directly associated with key strategy elements.

Question 3: Is a new approach or change to our existing assumptions, plans, or expectations necessary?

Is there evidence of the need to question strategy viability and consider new options?

- Essential factors enumerated in the "working or viable strategy" section above are missing or not satisfied.
- Feasibility is uncertain, or confidence in existing strategies and plans is lacking.

Question 4: Does a needed or revised set of initiatives suggest that re-articulation of our core strategy is necessary?

Is re-articulation of or additions to our stated strategy necessary?

- We require significant new actions which change how we should describe the firm's future direction and actions.
- We require significant changes to capital structure (leveraging, de-leveraging, follow-on stock offering, spin-off, strategic partnerships, etc.).

Asking these testing-for-strategy questions and summarizing the responses for the executive team adds an important dimension to the common fact base that is extremely valuable to have early in the strategic planning process. Shared knowledge of the critical facts provides a useful platform from which to approach strategic decision making. We will revisit these questions in more detail after discussing the model in its entirety.

Risk & Uncertainty as Strategic Planning Considerations

All plans for the future rely on assumptions, projections, or predictions. In a June 2000 article, Courtney, Kirkland, and Viguerie confirm this by stating:

> *At the heart of the traditional approach to strategy lies the assumption that executives, by applying a set of powerful analytic tools can predict the future of any business accurately enough to choose a clear strategic direction for it. The process often involves underestimating uncertainty in order to lay out a vision of future events sufficiently precise to be captured in a discounted-cash-flow (DCF) analysis. When the future is truly uncertain, this approach is at best marginally helpful and at worst downright dangerous: underestimating uncertainty can lead to strategies that neither defend a company against the threats nor take advantage of the opportunities that higher levels of uncertainty provide. Another danger lies at the other extreme: if managers can't find a strategy that works under traditional analysis, they may abandon the analytical rigor of their planning process altogether and base their decisions on gut instinct.*[2]

The authors go on to specify four levels of "residual uncertainty" under which strategic planning often takes place. These range from "clear enough future" to "true uncertainty."

While in the throes of strategic planning, you can create risk in essentially two ways – making poor strategic decisions or not making strategic decisions at all. Most firms eventually succeed at committing both of these errors. Since few are exempt from such common errors, some basic risk categories are worth keeping in mind as strategy development progresses.

Risk 1: Emerging Technologies & Innovative Companies

Phil Simon, author of several books on how technology impacts business, sees *risk aversion* as a serious impediment that plagues many established companies. "For every Google, Amazon or Facebook taking major risks, hundreds of large companies are still playing it safe," he says. "Today, the costs of inaction almost always exceed the costs of action."

For example, a company called ThirdLove is now selling ladies' bras in ½ cup size increments exclusively online (something not normally available in department stores). A key part of their offering is an "accurate bra fitting at home without being prodded by a stranger." ThirdLove has a sizing app that turns your smartphone into a "virtual measuring tape." Snap a few quick photos, and it figures out exactly what size you are, down to the half cup. (Likewise, a purveyor of men's custom shirts called MTaylor has a similar iPhone app and customer offering.)

Clearly ThirdLove represents a new business model that disrupts not only traditional ladies' garment makers, but brick and mortar retailers as well. How should players in these industries react? Or should they? Later, we go into more depth on the importance of business model examination.

So be aware that many of the threats facing businesses today are *digital* threats and that they may be coming from outside your industry.

A recent PWC survey[3] reveals that:

> *Digital transformation is both a challenge and an opportunity. Digitization has blurred or even eliminated rigid industry boundaries starting with the media, content, and communications industries and*

is now spreading everywhere. The new digital business world has no pre-defined boundaries, no industry-based rules or limitations.

Indeed, 54% of CEOs have entered a new sector or sub-sector, or considered it, in the past three years, according to PwC. More than half (56%) of CEOs think it likely that companies will increasingly compete in new industries over the next three years. Unlike in the past, when unrelated diversification was the business strategy of only large conglomerates, PwC found that 51% of the smaller firms (revenues up to $100 million) included in the survey, have entered a new sector or subsector, or considered doing so, within the past three years, compared with 64% of the largest firms, with revenues of over $10 billion.

What technologies do CEOs think are the most strategic in facilitating the digital transformation of their companies and industries? Leading the list are:

- *Mobile technologies for customer engagement (81%)*
- *Data mining and analysis (80%)*
- *Cyber security (78%)*
- *The Internet of Things or IOT (65%)*
- *Socially enabled business processes (61%)*
- *Cloud computing (60%)*

Most interesting here is the inclusion of the Internet of Things, somewhat new on the scene as a business buzzword, but it's possible that the survey respondents have either referred to what they see as its future potential or to the value they have already derived from established technologies such as RFID and machine-to-machine communications.[4]

Risk 2: Risk of Value Destruction

In an effort to pursue new directions and strategies, is it possible to diminish the value of the existing business? A retail convenience store operator wanted to diversify and expand its offering to customers. The operator decided its forward plan would include a sizeable program in which it would demolish existing small convenience stores (which were virtually all company owned) and replace them with larger format stores to drive higher same store sales in these locations. But an alternative strategy – to open more new locations – could be shown to add significantly more incremental revenues, profits, and cash flows. The first option – called "razing and rebuilding" – would have consumed almost as much capital as a completely new site. However, with only a relatively minor portion of the post-project sales being incremental to pre-project sales, returns would be far weaker (and in most cases negative). Such a course of action would inefficiently consume capital resources and reduce the company's value in the financial markets. In contrast, building the new formats on new properties would result in meaningful new sources of revenue, increasing the company's valuation.

Why was the company considering a large-scale raze and rebuild program? First, diversifying the company's offering was a strategic objective, and this course of action would support this objective. Second, the company found it difficult to obtain attractive properties in the way it had been doing for years. Desirable opportunities seemed more difficult to come by. So consider the dilemma: Be proactive and follow a course of action which seemingly supports the company's strategic objectives or *do nothing* and *appear* to have a worse story to tell the world. In this particular case, doing nothing and avoiding value destruction turned out to be superior to a seemingly proactive action apparently consistent with stated strategic objectives. When a CEO talks to the market, he or she likes to tout what they are or will be *doing* – not what they will *not* be doing. Choosing a potentially more valuable and correct *status quo* option in the short term may take more courage and conviction about the ultimate objectives of a company. The goal after all is to preserve or create more shareholder value.

This example of a company struggling to make the right decision demonstrates the risk of not clearly defining in advance specific, meaningful criteria for deciding between strategic options. A corollary to strategic decision criteria would be to consider the possible justifications for not applying your pre-determined criteria.

ExxonMobil, for example, has a reputation for committing to relatively few bad or unprofitable capital projects. Why? Because they use strict criteria to guide their internal decision making process. They are willing to say "no" to any project that doesn't meet their criteria, one of their most well-known being the monetization of enormous natural gas resources associated with the famous oil field in Prudhoe Bay, Alaska. For decades, ExxonMobil has considered every conceivable option for bringing this gas to market, but no option has ever satisfied their criteria for project sanction. Exxon is a very financially conservative company with a AAA credit rating, something they consider strategically important. The projects they undertake, along with the accompanying investment decisions, are enormous. Likewise, the magnitude of a single bad decision to invest in a new project is just as enormous.

Those intimately familiar with Discounted Cash Flow analysis may be thinking, "But they're hurting Net Present Value (NPV) by delaying projects until all investment criteria have been met." But consider this: A project (in its entirety) which will have a positive NPV when undertaken in the future, will still have a positive NPV today, although the NPV may be relatively small. On the other hand, an ill-conceived project, one which ultimately proves to generate negative NPV, will be even more costly from a present value perspective if the firm rushes ahead to do it now. Exxon is very clear about its investment criteria and patiently waits until the conditions are right to invest.

Risk 3: Making False Assumptions

Errors and oversights in scanning the environment can lead to the costly, untoward effects of strategies based on false or erroneous assumptions. One way to avoid such errors is to ask ourselves at this stage, "What is it we know that isn't so?" For example, a company *believed* they had certain cost advantages which were never really proven or demonstrated numerically. One executive said, "On the contrary, we could see no real advantage in the numbers at all." A false narrative was being perpetuated; whether this was intentional or unintentional was beside the point.

To avoid false assumptions, we can solicit input from a cross section of the organization's employees. This input can be an important step in gathering and validating data about the environment (internal and external) in which the business is operating. Securing input from people across a broad spectrum of organizational functions and levels goes a long way toward preventing a myopic view of the landscape.

Sometimes, in order to challenge false assumptions and beliefs, it's necessary to directly expose and confront them. For example, in one organization we are aware of, participants in their planning process were asked and specifically assigned to articulate and discuss what they experience in their business as typical completions of these phrases:

"We must …"
"We can't …"
"We always …"
"We never …"

Discussing statements like these can reveal much about the beliefs people have about the organization's inherent biases, characteristics, and culture. Data collected during these discussions can help identify themes that strategic planners need to be aware of and take into consideration during the planning process. Planners can investigate major themes to ascertain their validity.

Using a "management hackathon" concept, a successful consumer-goods company recently involved its entire organization in an open-source strategy process. The "hackathon" can be described as an integrated, multistage platform that allows participants to discuss ideas, express opinions, and contribute expertise collectively. This effort started with an organization-wide online discussion about risks to the company's growth engine. Risks discussed included everything from higher input costs, stagnant industry growth, and a growing competitive threat from imitators to certain products and the business model. Using a combination of in-person meetings and workshops, as well as online channels, these gathered risks then formed the basis for a bottom-up process that spawned over a thousand new strategic insights.

These insights were aggregated into roughly ten strategic themes – from reengineering the retail experience and digital technology to creating service ecosystems around the company's strongest brands. All employees were asked, via an online platform, to provide a rank order for these insights and to suggest specific business ideas embodying them. The input helped management narrow the strategic themes down to three and to identify several high-priority opportunities.[5]

Risk 4: Failure to Allocate Funding for the Future

Strategic planning is often confused or intertwined with the annual budgeting cycle. Executives make key decisions at a certain time of year so that next year's budget can reflect decisions and needs for the upcoming year. One of the major risks to such a budget-focused approach to planning is that you may fail to anticipate what must be done or invested in now to address medium-term imperatives or strategic actions which will largely be executed two to four years out.

Typically the finance department leads the budgeting process and assembles annual budgets. Since many executives detest budgeting, most find nothing wrong with this from an operating budget point of view. But what about from a strategic, longer-range perspective? The annual budget is often developed with little or no inclusion of strategic plan inputs and is typically *incremental* in nature rather than being strategically driven. Who then will be available and accountable for reconciling and balancing financial commitments for both the operating and strategic investments the organization will make? How will the organization decide when operational and strategic priorities conflict with the financial resources available to fund them? Such decisions require perspective from both operating and strategic vantage points. This in turn suggests that the CFO or other senior financial executives should be actively involved in the strategic planning process.

Later, we discuss Strategic Initiative Formation where strategic initiatives are the primary vehicles for executing on the organization's strategic imperatives and goals. A major criterion for determining whether a set of actions rises to the level of a strategic initiative is its funding profile over the period of time that will be required to successfully complete it. Strategic initiatives are essentially bets on the future needed to assure the forward success of the business. They sometimes represent a single budget cycle but just as often can span multiple budget cycles.

Chapter 3 – Common Fact Base Development
Key Thoughts & Takeaways

Before proceeding to the next chapter, please take a few minutes to think about the following with your organization in mind:

What are my key takeaways from this chapter?

What issues have I observed in my company or organization?

What are the implications for my organization?

4. Business Model Assessment

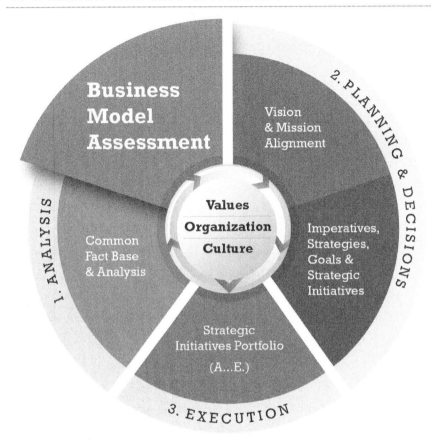

When faced with a choice between changing and proving there's no need to change, most people get busy on the proof.
— John Kenneth Galbraith

Rearranging the Deck Chairs

Having a healthy, robust business model with which to operate and upon which to base the future seems a rather obvious condition for a successful enterprise. Yet, time and again we watch companies struggle to find plausible causes for their most severe business issues. Surprisingly often, they are literally and simply unable to recognize (or admit to) a faulty, declining business model. Rather than even considering the possibility that their company's model may be failing, leaking, becoming less competitive, under attack, or simply outmoded, executives not uncommonly misread the undoing of a historically successful business model. Instead, they attribute root causes of decline to more mundane problems. They point to things like sales organization effectiveness, poor marketing, key staffing issues, faulty organization structure, competitive pressure, poor business environment, and so on.

As an essential step in the strategic planning process, executives need to pause long enough to take a fresh look at the firm's fundamental business model – as it was, as it is, and how it should be evolving. Any business model needs to evolve for the business to not only survive today, but prosper and grow tomorrow. This evaluation should take place before setting strategic goals. Failure to perform such a vital self-examination may do more to put a business at risk long term than any other missed step. Consider the once-successful business models of Kodak, Blockbuster, and AOL.

Fixes vs. Solutions

We frequently see executives attempting to *fix* any number of issues – sometimes *anything but* the real problem – before they begin to consider facing the more fundamental task of assessing the health of their firm's business model. Among the more frequent *fixes* we see attempted are:

- Reorganizing the sales force

- Changing the sales compensation system
- Making management team changes
- Terminating the [ops, strategy, sales...] executive
- Raising or lowering prices
- Refocusing marketing efforts
- Replacing the ad agency (a.k.a. blaming a partner)
- Cutting costs
- Outsourcing [manufacturing, HR, IT...], at times without any evidence that the outsourcing firm is better or cheaper
- Centralizing or de-centralizing business divisions
- Recapitalizing or other significant changes to capital structure
- Consolidating operations
- Announcing layoffs
- Pursuing questionable acquisition and divestiture actions
- Replacing the CEO or division executives

While these actions may or may not have a beneficial effect on a declining business, the one thing they *do* have in common is that they will fail to accomplish meaningful improvement if not done in concert with more fundamental changes to the company's business model – if in fact the business model is where the core issue exists.

Business model slippage is likely to be characterized by warning signals like:

- Defection of key distributors or customers
- Declining profit margins
- Market share stagnation
- Defection of key employees
- New technologies being employed by competitors (but not by your firm)

- Lack of new products
- Tired, outmoded, or dingy facilities or other tangible assets
- Declining *esprit-de-corps* among workers
- Disruption by new entrants into your historical marketplace
- Protect vs. grow mentality or risk aversion
- Predictability of existing revenue streams declining

What Is a Business Model?

What then is a business model and how can you both define and optimize it? In simple terms, a business model comprises two elements or characteristics which we believe should be inseparable:

1. How a firm monetizes its business processes, technologies, and products or services to create sustainable or repeatable levels of:
   - Margin and profit
   - Business growth
2. How a firm creates competitive advantage by means of a differentiated value proposition:
   - *As perceived by* the firm's customers
   - To the benefit of its equity owners

The power of a successful business model lies in the *combined* effect of these two simple elements. Many indicators, signs, and symptoms point to a healthy (or conversely, a declining) business model. But the fatal flaw of too many businesses rests in their inability to recognize and begin seriously dealing with the signs and symptoms of business model decay before it is already too late to change.

If there is a fundamental concept to understand regarding successful business models, it may be the construct of Customer Perceived Value and its expression by means of this equation:

$$\text{Customer Perceived Value} = \frac{\text{Quality} + \text{Utility}}{\text{Price}}$$

The concept of *shifting perceptions of value and utility* by customers is central to developing an understanding of how business models succeed and fail – how they rise and fall. The fact that customer perceptions of value can turn on a dime when we least expect it accounts for failure on the part of many businesses and executive teams. The signs and signals of shifting value, whether perceived or real, in the market place are overlooked at our peril.

For an in-depth discussion of the importance of understanding value-changing factors and the relationships between them as they pertain to business models, we can look to *Winning the Race for Value: Strategies to Create Competitive Advantage* by Sheehy, Bracey, and Frazier. They describe value migration in this way:

> As value moves from one business model to another, it slowly unhinges the old order. Whatever the causes of the value shift, such as demographics, economic cycles, deregulation, or social attitudes, the business environment changes dramatically. Profit margins head south, and in time, investment capital flows out. Slowly, imperceptibly, the old, successful model of the past becomes less and less functional. Most are too busy perfecting the old model to notice. There is a nagging feeling that something is wrong, but few can articulate the problem. This is the moment of truth for the institution and its leadership. If the organization is to survive, it must now move in bold, new directions. Unfortunately, if history is any guide, most fail this important test.[1]

John H. Dobbs (co-author of this book) states the following in a white paper titled, "Competition's New Battleground: The Integrated Value Chain":

> *Value chain leaders create new business models to offer a new way to deliver value to customers. These leaders focus first on the market and the customer, discovering how the customer wants to do business and creating new or improved value propositions accordingly. Businesses can no longer ignore the wants and needs of the marketplace and hope to survive. Someone will emerge to fill the customer's unmet needs, often by offering a product or service the customer didn't even know was possible. Customers – whether consumer or business-to-business – will always act out of self-interest. They will behave in accordance with the "Customer Perceived Value" equation [shown above]. [2]*

New business models and value chains can rapidly change the landscape of an entire industry. Jack Ma, executive chairman of Alibaba Group, says that China's middle class (which barely existed 20 years ago) is now equal to the entire U.S. population and is expected to double within seven years. Alibaba now has more than 350 million annual active buyers in its ecosystem. In 2013, for example, farmers in the U.S. Pacific Northwest sold 180 tons of cherries to China via the Alibaba platform. It set off a cherry frenzy in China and sales in 2014 more than tripled to 600 tons. [3] We'll look at more about Alibaba's vision for the future in a later chapter.

Other Definitions for Business Models

A variety of other definitions can be found for business models. Harvard Business School's Clayton Christensen suggests that a business model should consist of four elements:

1. Customer Value Proposition
2. Profit Formula
3. Key Resources
4. Key Processes

These elements are not incompatible with our proposed definition above.

Christensen was an early thought leader on the business impact of disruptive technologies and strategies. In his book, *The Innovator's Dilemma: The Revolutionary Book That Will Change the Way You Do Business*, he says:

> *The innovator's task is to ensure that his innovation – the disruptive technology that doesn't make sense – is taken seriously within the company without putting at risk the needs of present customers who provide profit and growth. The problem can be resolved only when new markets are considered and carefully developed around new definitions of value.*

Once again, the topic of value becomes central to how business models are viewed and defined.

In a January 2011 HBR article, Casadesus-Masanell and Ricart state that "Companies make three types of choices when creating business models: Policy Choices, Asset Choices, and Governance Choices." Results or consequences then emerge from these choices creating "virtuous cycles of success that are self-reinforcing."

How Wide Is Your Moat?

Since medieval times, moats have been constructed to surround and protect a castle or fort. For several years, the financial analysis firm Morningstar has used a framework of wider and narrower "economic moats" to inform their subscribers. Their service offers a more objective tool to assist with identification of businesses that may have a wider (or narrower) moat of protection shielding their business model from impending decay and competition.

In the book *Why Moats Matter: The Morningstar Approach to Stock Investing,* Morningstar's Heather Brilliant and Elizabeth Collins suggest that the concept of "economic moats" helps investors find superior businesses and determine when to buy them in order to maximize returns over the long term. Companies with economic moats are viewed as "great businesses that can fend off competition and earn high returns on capital for many years."[4]

To determine a company's economic moat rating, the Morningstar approach begins by asking two questions:

1. Are the company's Returns on Invested Capital (ROIC) likely to exceed its Weighted Average Cost of Capital (WACC) in the future?

2. Does the company appear to have at least one of the five sources of "sustainable competitive advantage" (intangible assets, cost advantage, switching costs, network effect, or efficient scale)?

If we think ROICs are likely to exceed WACC in the future and the company appears to have any of the five sources of competitive advantage, it's possible that the firm does indeed have a wide economic moat. But the investigation doesn't stop there. We next assess the company's ability to generate positive economic profits 10 to 20 years into the future. *In free-market economies, rivals will eventually encroach on any excess profits earned by companies **without protective moats**.* Time and capital requirements aren't effective barriers to entry when we have a long-term time horizon. Some companies may generate positive ROIC-WACC spreads today and for a few years into the future. But if their competitive advantages aren't sustainable enough, competitors will begin to eat into excess profits over time.

In 2011, Morningstar initiated an Exchange Traded Fund called Market Vectors Morningstar Wide Moat ETF (MOAT) based on its philosophy of favoring companies characterized with a wide moat, multiple sources of competitive advantage, and potential for ROIC to exceed WACC. While the fund is obviously subject to the same vagaries of the market as any others, it has managed to beat the S&P 500 over that same time period. For 37 of the past 38 five-year rolling periods, this ETF index fund has beaten the S&P 500. In July 2015 Morningstar also introduced a MOAT type fund for international markets with the "MOTI" symbol.

One of the things that can help create a wider moat that is less susceptible to attack from competitors is proprietary data or analytics that competitors do not possess. In his new book management guru Ram Charan asserts:

> *The single greatest instrument of change in today's business world and the one that is creating major uncertainties for an ever-growing universe of companies, is the advancement of mathematical algorithms and their related sophisticated software. Never before has so much artificial mental power been available to so many – power to deconstruct and predict patterns and changes in everything from consumer behavior to the maintenance requirements and operating lifetimes of industrial machinery. In combination with other technological factors – including broadband mobility, sensors, and vastly increased data crunching capacity – algorithms are dramatically changing both the structure of the global economy and the nature of business.*[5]

Think about how Netflix has used its proprietary algorithms and the internet to dominate the video rental and streaming business, while driving established companies like Blockbuster out of business. In the early 2000s before Netflix was an industry leader, Reed Hastings of Netflix had several discussions with Blockbuster CEO John Antioco to see if the video chain would be interested in purchasing its DVD-by-mail company for $50 million. Antioco passed, thinking there would never be a substantial market for such a model and said the asking price was too high. Today, Netflix has a market cap of $25 billion, and Blockbuster is nothing but a memory. Blockbuster is trying to revive its business by partnering with NCR to distribute DVDs through the Red Box machines that are becoming increasingly popular. Perhaps NCR and Blockbuster can disrupt Netflix?

Witness also how Uber and VRBO are using technology enabled algorithms to disrupt the hotel, taxi cab, and limo industries. Uber is upending the taxi business with an app to connect passengers with rides and a proprietary algorithm that, in part, governs surge pricing. Surge pricing raises fares at times of heavy demand. Uber is working on a global policy to cap prices in times of disaster or emergency. These examples of emerging business models did not even exist a few years ago.

Better the Disrupter than the Disrupted

The biggest problem facing CEOs today is the pace and intensity of business-model disruption, says David Hughes, Chairman and CEO of Silver Peak Systems. Cloud and mobile technology innovation are making it easier for new entrants to develop entirely fresh and unexpected business models, which are disrupting not only the technology sector, but virtually every industry.

For instance, as mobile phone applications consume more of people's time, they spend less time doing things like watching television. Phones and addictive apps like games are not really direct competition for TV production companies or TV manufacturers, but they are impacting those markets. Even regulated industries are being forced to adapt. It would seem the scale and scope of change being forced on large established businesses is occurring at an unprecedented pace.[6]

Companies need to be constantly scanning the horizon for new competitors who may be emerging with technology driven disruptive business models. An emerging competitor and disruptor for Lowe's and Home Depot is a startup called BuildDirect. "Building a better model with a focus on data and logistics, BuildDirect has constructed an online platform for low-cost building materials." The Vancouver, British Colombia-based company is forging direct connections between manufacturers and end customers (DIY homeowners and contractors) while reducing costs. Their e-commerce platform allows consumers and contractors to order directly from manufacturers rather than through middlemen like Home Depot.

With lower shipping costs and no handoffs, BuildDirect was able to offer consumers savings of up to 80%. Their revenue grew from $1 million to $14 million from their first year to the next and now stands at $150 million. They plan to grow to $1 billion or more. Fifty-seven percent of their revenue comes from repeat business and referrals. They now have 10 warehouses so they can offer delivery on bulk orders within 48 hours. Many of their manufacturers are holding inventory on consignment in the BuildDirect warehouses because they have a more predictable supply chain using the BuildDirect e-commerce platform.[7]

Even early-generation technology companies are now being disrupted by superior or different business models. Startup VarageSale competes with Craigslist and has raised $34 million in venture funding. According to Bloomberg.com, "VarageSale is one of a few startups taking on a difficult mission: unseating Craigslist as king of local e-commerce. The Craigslist site looks like it hasn't had a fresh coat of paint since the mid-1990s when Craig Newmark created it in San Francisco. It doesn't incorporate social media services, and most listings on its mobile version are cut and tough to read.

"A former kindergarten teacher and her husband, who had an antispam company created the VarageSale mobile app that allows people to sell their junk easily from a mobile phone, and it lets people connect through their Facebook profiles. VerageSale is now operating in all provinces of Canada and in 42 US states."[8]

Where's the CIO's Business Model Input?

Given the fact that tomorrow's business models are more likely to be technology related (or disrupted by new technology), in many organizations a critical input is missing from the executive team doing the strategic planning – input from the CIO.

A 2014 survey of more than 700 executives, of which more than half have a technology role or focus, showed that only about "one third of their CIO's are very or extremely involved in shaping the overall business strategy and agenda. Only half say their CIO is even on their organization's most senior teams." The study concludes that "there is little awareness of or agreement on how IT can meaningfully shape a business's future."[9] How unfortunate, given the increasing role of technology in changing, improving, or disrupting business models.

The CIO and staff, including business partners and vendors can make valuable contributions to technology for enabling the business and accessing new markets. Of course, this also means that the CIO must bring valuable input to the table and not focus solely on the technical infrastructure supporting the business. In many startup businesses, the IT expertise resides with a business founder, making the founder a de-facto CIO or CTO and senior officer combined.

Some companies are going to great lengths to become more open to innovation and emerging technologies. To stay better abreast of technologies affecting their industry, in 2013, the giant UK supermarket chain Tesco set up an investment unit, Dunnhumby Ventures, to incubate fledgling tech companies. Tesco benefits by, for example, getting to try out new wearable technology to make warehouses more efficient. Other Dunnhumby clients include Coca-Cola, Pepsico, Kraft, T-Mobile, and L'Oreal.[10]

BNY Mellon recently opened a Silicon Valley office to focus on innovation. So did AstraZeneca. By making such moves, non-IT companies gain access to brand new technology (and entrepreneurial talent) while stopping short of buying technology startups outright.

Merck & Company, using a McKinsey management framework called Three Horizons, is assessing potential new areas for growth without neglecting performance in the present. Working on the third of the three horizons (products that will drive revenue in the future), Merck has now developed semantic analysis technologies that can discover intellectual property leakage and counterfeiting. Merck is turning this counterfeit discovery capability into an independent business (called Steelgate Intelligence Systems) serving the pharmaceutical industry and potentially companies in other markets that sell expensive goods. By looking beyond its existing business model, Merck may take advantage of a market need or adjacency that can extend its historical model and approach to the market.[11]

An indication of the growing importance technology holds for changing business models is the fact that corporate boards are beginning to create technology committees alongside their compensation and audit committees. "Corporate boards waking up to headlines about major security breaches are asking more pointed questions about company technology strategies and vulnerabilities."[12] Other firms address technology-deficient boards of directors by creating digital advisory boards or panels. An informal and smaller version of the corporate board, a digital advisory panel helps management stay atop trends in social media, big data, and digital commerce. According to the global board practice leader for executive recruiter Egon Zehnder, at least 50 Fortune 500 companies have set up such boards in the past 5 years.[13]

Given the potentially serious repercussions of inadequate assessments of value shifts and business model degradation, you may find it helpful to consider a range of questions that business leaders can ask themselves as they prepare for their responsibilities in strategic planning and decision making.

What Questions…

What Questions Should Executives Be Asking at the Business Model Stage of the Strategic Planning Process?

To objectively assess the condition of a company's business model, you must be prepared to not only ask, but also answer, a series of questions regarding the firm's existing business model from multiple perspectives. The questions that need to be answered at this stage in the planning process will reveal the relative health or weakness of the existing model when evaluated in light of our definitions of the:

- Elements of a successful Business Model
- Equation for Customer-Perceived Value

Both were introduced and explained earlier in this chapter.

Customer Perceived Value, Value Proposition, & Competitive Advantage Issues

1. How do customers describe us?
2. Is our business model:
   a. Emerging and growing?
   b. Established and maintaining?
   c. Outmoded and declining?
3. Can we succinctly describe the value proposition we provide to our customers?
4. How and to where is value migrating within our industry?
5. What do we see as our competitive advantage(s)?

6. How can we change the rules of the game in our industry to gain a *sustainable* competitive advantage?

7. Is our business model sustainable in the longer term? What signs of erosion do we see? Are our revenue streams becoming less predictable?

8. Is our business model (or industry) being disrupted? By whom? From where?

9. What is happening to our market share?

10. Which market trends are we reacting to? Which are we creating?

11. Which business and social ecosystems are we (or could we be) a part of?

12. What are we best known for? Are we best known for who or what we really are?

13. What percent of our business is repeat business?

14. Are we a leader or a follower?

15. Do we possess the right people and skills to improve our business model?

16. What competitive advantages are embedded in our business processes?

17. Does our workforce represent a competitive advantage? Why or why not? How do we measure employee engagement and morale?

18. Is our financial value being recognized and rewarded in the financial markets?

19. Have we translated our plans into numerical forecasts far enough into the future that we can confirm whether our current portfolio and known opportunities will together

deliver minimally required future value (i.e. equity appreciation equals or exceeds the cost of equity)?

Process, Product, Technology, & Efficiency Issues

1. What are our key or core business processes? How efficient are they? What is being done to improve them? What benchmarking have we done?

2. Are we better at: Innovation? Customer service? Low cost or low price? Quality?

3. Are we growing organically or externally?

4. Are our profit margins growing or declining?

5. Are our products or services being cannibalized? By whom or by what technology?

6. How do we make money? How sustainable and repeatable is our ability to monetize our business processes?

7. Which technologies are we lacking that would strengthen or enable our business model? What technology issues are holding us back?

8. Are there emerging technologies for which we have avoided defining a response or plan?

9. Are we under attack by a lower cost provider?

10. What percentage of our customers are unprofitable?

11. What share of our business is the result of innovation?

12. How do we compare financially to our competitors? To other companies of our size?

13. How often do we reorganize or change our organization structure? Why?

Certainly, other questions might be asked to evaluate a company's business model. These include questions that would be meaningful to a particular organization or its industry. As a major element of a strategic planning process, define the relevant questions in advance for your company and review them systematically with the executive team.

Many organizations have never discussed in a meaningful way the nature and characteristics of their business model. This is a major oversight, if not an outright strategic planning error. Understanding and proactively *managing* the firm's business model should be viewed as an important precursor to any effort to set strategies and goals for the future.

Defining (or Re-Thinking) a Business Model

As illustrated above, many questions can be asked to assess the condition, strengths, and weaknesses of an existing business model. Regardless of the condition of the business model, serious exploration of these questions puts executives engaged in strategic planning in a position to address bottom-line, business model questions:

1. What are the implications for us of not making any changes (or of making only minor incremental changes) to our current business model for growth and manner of doing business?

2. How must our business model and our operational capabilities be different in the future to create more value for both customers and shareholders?

3. How will our business model for planned growth be different than that of our existing core business?

4. What will change in the level or type of value perceived by our customers as a result of changes we will make to our company's business model?

With these questions in mind, the executive team can plan for potential changes to the business model. Failure to address these questions head on may indicate that executives have not analyzed the existing business model sufficiently or over a sufficiently long time horizon.

More about Evolving Business Models

In his book *Exponential Organizations: Why new organizations are ten times better, faster, and cheaper than yours (and what to do about it),* Salim Ismail, founding director of Singularity University, pulls no punches in delivering his answer. According to Ismail, large corporate structures are generally ill-equipped to identify and harness exponentials for competitive advantage; thus, they are at serious risk of being disrupted – even to the point of destruction – by small, more nimble startups. Furthermore, he believes CIOs working for these large companies have "the hardest job in corporate America today" because they must simultaneously drive innovation and keep their organization's assets and data secure.[14]

"Exponentials" are accelerating technologies for which performance relative to cost and size is doubling every one to two years – a rate similar to Moore's Law. It comes down to whether a given technology is both information-based and doubling steadily in its price performance. For example, in neuroscience the resolution of brain imaging is doubling about every eighteen months. Sensors and drones are doubling in price performance every nine months – an astounding pace – and solar energy has price performance doubling every twenty-two to thirty months. Exponential technologies have the power to shift value and thus accelerate the creation (or destruction) of business models.

Futurist Thornton May supports our admonition to ask the right questions at each stage of the strategic planning process and to not avoid asking questions about the state or health of the firm's business model. Says May:

Nokia was a 60% market-share leader in a highly technology-intensive business. The consumer phone industry was characterized by high fixed costs and high returns to scale, and was highly regulated, fully global and complex. And yet in less than five years, a competitor with no phone experience came to dominate the global market. Nokia, I think it is safe to assume, did not ask the right questions about the future. Its leaders understood technology trajectories but seemed to miss the point of technology transition, that it is critically important to differentiate between technology trajectory stories and technology transition realities.[15]

The now huge startup, Uber, is a major case in point for the difference between technology transition and trajectory. Uber's vision and business model are already guiding the $400 million company into new or adjacent markets beyond its current UberX ride share service. Recognizing that Uber has more than 200,000 active drivers (roughly double the size of the delivery workforce of United Parcel Service – UPS) Uber has been trying to build what its CEO has called an "urban logistics fabric." This fabric would extend Uber's business model to include:

- UberX – Rides with non-professional drivers
- UberRUSH – One hour package delivery
- UberEATS – Hot meals delivered from local restaurants
- UberPOOL – Low priced rides shared with strangers
- UberCARGO – Vans for moving furniture or individual possessions

Describing Uber's vision, CEO Travis Kalanick "sees in Uber the potential for a smoothly functioning instant-gratification economy, powered by the smartphone as the remote control for life. If we can get you a car in five minutes, we can get you anything in five minutes."

The Uber vision and business model have generated both rapid business growth and very high levels of interest in the investment community. The Wall Street Journal has previously reported that Uber may now be worth more than 120 times its trailing revenue. This revenue multiple may be a reflection of Uber's faster growth potential. Uber told some investors it expects revenue to grow 400% to $2 billion this year. Investors in Uber are enthusiastic about the potential, valuing the private company at $41 billion in its last funding round. Uber has matched an aggressive expansion into some 250 markets around the globe with a ferocious fundraising machine, securing more than $5 billion in debt and equity from investors in the 5 years since launching.[16]

As a new company, Uber's business model will certainly evolve, as both regulation and competition impact the business. For example, a California court has recently ruled that Uber's drivers are employees, not independent contractors. The impact of such forces on Uber's business model are difficult to predict. But one thing is certain, as Uber grows and continues to define itself, the business models of some of its competitors will need to be re-thought as well.

In April 2018, Uber acquired for $100 million a company called Jump Bikes. Uber has announced plans to integrate bike- and scooter-sharing services on its app, an acknowledgment that cars aren't always the best form of urban transport. The company has reportedly begun engineering its own electric scooter to compete with scooter companies Bird Rides and Lime. Jump Bikes is overseeing the electric scooter project. Of course, Uber is also engaged in the development of self-driving cars and flying taxis. Who knows what's next?

Companies like Uber and Apple are adept at viewing their business models as self-reinforcing, evolving ecosystems that take advantage of profitable adjacencies and market opportunities. Piece by piece, Apple proactively built a highly disruptive ecosystem. It attacked a fragmented, stale industry with superior technology providing a service that was more nimble, immediate, and hip (with its iPod). They expanded and bundled this service with additional lines of business (mobile) and provided (and control) a centralized catalog and ordering service to make buying others' products and services more convenient to the customer (the Apple app store). Think about how convenient the app store is for the customer. Imagine if you had to find out about each app available for the iPhone from each individual company that produces the app, and you had to register and pay for each company's product on their site rather than Apple's. Far fewer apps would be sold, and the iPhone would not have been so compelling to the consumer who was not already a die-hard Apple fan.

Self-Correcting Business Models?

A Peter Drucker maxim was that "any business enterprise has two – and only two – basic functions: marketing and innovation."

Innovation occurs mostly at the edges of a business, but we believe it much more powerful to innovate at its core. Improving a business by improving or reinventing its business model can pay huge dividends.

In an August 20, 2018 *Wall Street Journal* editorial titled, "Models Will Run the World," venture capitalists Steven Cohen and Matthew Granade contend that most industry-leading companies today are (or are becoming) software companies. They cite that long-term industry leaders like Aptiv and Domino's Pizza have adopted software to maintain or extend their competitive dominance. According to Cohen and Granade, "We believe a new more powerful business model has evolved from its software predecessor. These companies structure their processes to put continuously learning models, built on "closed loop" data, at the center of what they do. When built right, they create a reinforcing cycle: their products get better, allowing them to collect more data, which allows them to built better models, making their products better, and onward. These are Model Driven Businesses. They are being created inside incumbents and startups across a range of industries."[17]

The authors contend that "there is no shortage of hype about artificial intelligence and big data, but models are the source of the real power behind these tools." The concept of a self-learning or self-improving model can be explained like this: a model is a decision framework in which the logic is derived by algorithm from data rather than explicitly programmed or implicitly conveyed via someone's intuition. The output is a prediction on which a decision can be made. Once created, a model can learn from its successes and failures with speed and sophistication not normally matched by humans. (We note here that according to IDC the large compound annual growth rate of spending forecasts for Artificial Intelligence between 2016 and 2021 is 46%.)

A model-driven business then uses models to power the key decisions in its business process, creating revenue streams, cost efficiencies, or service improvements. Building such a system requires a mechanism (often software-based) to collect data, processes to create models from the data, the models themselves, and a mechanism (also typically software based) to deliver or act on the suggestions from those models. A model-driven business creates a system built around continuously improving models that define the business. In a data-driven business, the data helps the business; in a model-driven business the models are the business in a virtual world.

Other examples of such model-driven businesses include Amazon, Monsanto, and Netflix.

- By 2013 an estimated 35% of Amazon revenue came from Amazon's product recommendations
- Monsanto models predict optimal places for farmers to plant, based on historical yields, satellite imagery, weather data, etc.

- The Netflix recommendation model is famous, driving 80% of content consumption, estimated to be worth more than $1 billion per year in revenue

The concept of an evolving, self-improving business model is real and should be considered both as an opportunity and as a potential threat as executives seek to assess and improve their company's business model. These new models can be hugely disruptive. CB Insights 2018 reports that 41% of executives say their companies are very or extremely at risk of disruption. Remember also that these new models don't necessarily have to be developed internally. Another 2018 Conference Board survey found that almost half (49%) of companies prefer to partner with innovators or acquire them, rather than building new capabilities for themselves. Monsanto, for example, acquired key elements of its technology from a $1.1 billion acquisition of The Climate Corp.

A self-improving, self-correcting business model should have a positive impact on the organization's ability to sustain or repeat and grow its business model over time. Later is this chapter, we discuss the concept and benefits of business model "balance."

A Bifurcated Business Model?

In this chapter, we have focused on stepping up to realistically assess the strengths and weaknesses of an organization's business model. Through this analysis, you may find more than one business model in operation – simultaneously. Consider this scenario:

Business Model 1

The first business model is the company's traditional or historical business, which in most cases represents the lion's share of the company's revenue and profit. Although the first business model may be in decline or losing competitive advantage in the marketplace, it's probably still the firm's profit engine, even if it's no longer the growth engine.

Business Model 2

The second business model is more likely an emerging business that is competing for resources and attention with the traditional business internally – and for a foothold in a new or adjacent market externally. The emerging business model may in fact be struggling to establish a beachhead in a new product category or with a different type of customer than the company's historical customer base. It may or may not have strong support across the organization.

In the event of such bifurcated business models operating in parallel (and there may be more than two concomitant models) the strategic planning process must take into account both models and provide strategic direction for both, individually – and in combination. Since the organization's results will be determined by the combined effects of both business models, over- or under-investing in either business model may be risky and short sighted. The rates of growth (or decline) of both business models must be considered and realistically anticipated if you are to optimize the strategic plan and the organization's results. Failure to identify real opportunities and subsequent failure to plan and resource adequately for the first business model in the medium term can be fatal.

For an interesting historical example of a successfully bifurcated business model, we again look to Apple. Known as Apple Computer and a relatively minor player in desktop computers, Apple began transforming itself with the introduction of the iPod and then the iPhone, competing with Sony, Nokia, and Motorola. Apple never stopped improving its computers and in fact has continued to improve market share and profit margins. But Apple also leveraged its core competencies of product and software design so well that they were able to enter markets which were at the time dominated by nontraditional competitors for Apple. Because of Apple's competencies, strategy, and leadership, their personal electronics now dominate the competition. Sony still struggles against Apple and competes well in other markets, but Nokia and Motorola barely exist today. Apple's computer and iPod business, though respected and still growing, is now dwarfed by the financial impact of the iPhone, making Apple one of the most valuable companies in the world.

A Business Model Value Creation Continuum

Apple's business model is also a good example of one that has evolved toward both greater business and customer value. The diagram below illustrates a way to think about the circumstance in which an emerging business model shifts toward the future, while at the same time the company also focuses on existing customers and generating profits from its traditional (and improving) operations.

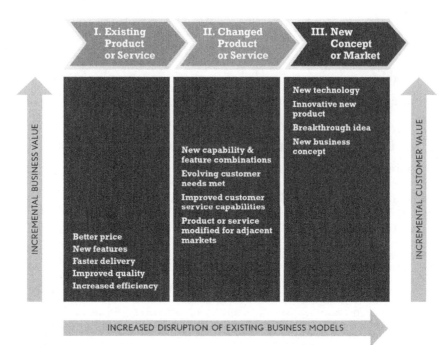

As the organization's business model is being assessed, think in terms of these three value creation continuum phases to draw conclusions and ideas about both where the company's business model is *now* and where it is *headed*. If the company's strategies and plans are currently limited to phases I or II, they are unlikely to create sufficient future opportunities to assure its success in the longer term.

McKinsey & Co. has described a five-step process for reframing beliefs about and then innovating business models.[18] The process includes:

1. Outlining the dominant business model in your industry
2. Dissecting the most important long-held belief into its supporting notions
3. Turning an underlying belief on its head
4. Sanity-testing your reframe
5. Translating the reframed belief into your industry's new business model

While these may or may not be the best steps to follow for new business model conceptualization, the important thing is to at least consider how a new business model might possibly emerge from your company and "change the game" in your industry.

Having said much about the importance of defining and pursuing a successful business model, we now want to consider the concept of a balanced business model.

Business Model *Balance* Matters

We theorize that virtually any business exhibits tendencies that will render it relatively balanced or unbalanced in terms of its strategic priorities or focus. Sustained, balanced business models are more likely to be successful over time than those that do not achieve balance or are not able to sustain a balanced focus over time. So what does balance mean?

Broadly, a company can focus its efforts toward three desirable outcomes:

- Growth
- Profitability
- Repeatability or sustainability

The prioritization of these objective outcomes can be looked at from the *extreme* perspectives of several types of companies typically concerned with one objective over the other two.

- Start-up company – growth
  - o Attain scale as quickly as possible
  - o Establish first mover market potential
  - o Establish audience or user base
- Large, mature company – profitability (potentially in a shrinking market)
  - o Maximizing returns of significant capitalization

- o Cost efficiency
- o Optimization of systems and processes
- Family-owned company – repeatability or sustainability
  - o Preserve income generation potential
  - o Preserve family legacy or image
  - o Preserve asset values for next generation

The truth is, that most businesses are not (or shouldn't be) exclusively in a grow-at-all-costs mode, nor in an extract-the-most-profits-now mode, nor in a be-around-another-a-hundred-years mode. Most businesses should be concerned with profitable operations and profitable growth, *repeatedly*. A natural speed limit, rhythm, pace, and cadence allows a company to focus on all three broad objectives appropriately and to make efficient use of its resources. For a company to continually create value for its equity holders and for its customers, it must operate a business model that allows it to at least somewhat balance these objectives. (For a detailed review of our rationale and financial assumptions in support of our Balanced Business Model theory see Appendix A.)

We assert that if a company's strategy and business model allows it to balance the three broad objectives, that company will be able to create greater value in the long term. In practice, what evidence supports this case? What is the theory behind this premise? Is there data to support this claim?

Fundamentally, in order to create value, a company must generate a profit – at an appropriately growing scale[*] – repeatedly. This is what a "going concern" does – it invests, and it generates a profit year after year. Ask yourself if you would be willing to invest personal money in a company that you were not sure would be profitable any time in the near future or would even be around in a few years. Certainly you wouldn't. You need to be able to see the

---

[*] Growth can be positive, flat, or even negative, thus, the modifier "appropriately growing."

company's potential, and a key to its potential is its profitable growth prospects far into the future. In short, this is the simple justification for our claim.

This simple argument, as well as the more mathematical argument in Appendix A, should be enough to establish the link between a balanced business model and business value. In terms of data, we will provide examples from select companies from a major industry.

Let's start with a basic orientation to help you understand these examples.

A Business Model that Balances Three Fundamental Objectives Creates Comparatively Greater Value Over Time

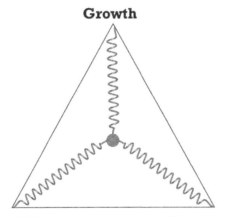

Growth

Profitability   **Repeatability**

Analyses we have conducted in different industries reveal that companies that are able to achieve balance between growth, profitability, and repeatability tend to create greater financial value over time. The three objectives, or areas of focus, of a company's activities are key to achieving the ultimate objective of value creation. But these areas of focus are often at odds with each other. For many businesses, it is much easier to focus on just one of the objectives than to create a business model, or way of doing business, which enables the company to accomplish all three.

Think of the company being attached to three "springs" – each pulling or maintaining tension in a different direction. At any one time, the company can focus its attention on one or all of the objectives, but undue focus on one (or neglect of the other two) comes at a cost.

You could also think of this model as someone spinning three plates on three rods trying to keep them all in motion and off the ground. Without a reasonably balanced effort between the plates, eventually one becomes wobbly and the spinner is forced to focus extra attention on the plate in danger of falling. The company cannot sustain its pursuit of value without having resources – systems, processes, people, and capital – allocated appropriately. If all resources are focused on just one objective or "flavor of the quarter," the other focus areas will almost surely suffer. And this is the key point: Apparent strength in *one* focus area is often just an illusion. In the long run, you either have balanced strength or unavoidable weakness in one or both of the other areas.

Imbalance Signals Weakness & Vulnerability

One Weakness   **Two Weaknesses**

A single focus area pursued to excess ultimately weakens a firm. Consider a hypothetical company in tension represented by the framework surrounding the springs. The position of the circle centered and attached to the springs represents the net focus of the company. At the beginning of this section, we illustrated a company with a balanced focus pulled by three springs of equal tension such that there are equal forces acting on the company's business dynamic. Now imagine one of the springs begins to lose tension. If two of the springs have retained their original tension while one has weakened, we would observe the condition shown to the left above. Not explicitly illustrated is the distortion in the framework the changing tension would cause. The two stronger springs exert forces not offset by the third, causing the framework to warp, resulting in a more precarious, unbalanced situation. If not corrected, the imbalance inevitably leads to a second spring losing its tension, causing even greater imbalance and framework distortion. If two springs become relatively weaker, the situation starts to look like illustration on the right above. Stresses continue to mount while taxing the organization's infrastructure and human resources, rendering the firm increasingly unable to operate in a balanced manner. Then, rather than being able to operate within an optimal range, the firm's executives are forced to run from one fire to the next. Performance suffers, value is destroyed, morale deteriorates, and people leave, looking for a less stressful environment.

Perhaps you are asking: "But what if a 'weak' spring is not actually weak, but rather, one or more of the other springs has been overly strengthened? Isn't that a good thing?" It's a valid question. After all, isn't it management's job to continually improve and shore up weaknesses – to make things better, not worse? The analogy would be to replace one of the original springs with a stronger spring. But when we do, the company that was formerly in equilibrium is pulled relatively toward the stronger spring. If this situation is not changed by replacing the other springs, they will over time lose their tension due to the force of the stronger spring, and the situation will create forces on the business framework in a manner similar to the condition caused by two weak springs. The imbalanced situation cannot be maintained forever. Management must eventually replace one or both of the other springs.

So how does this relate to a real company? The classic example of business model imbalance is often found in an organization characterized by a management team which has a singular focus on growth ... perhaps even the need to grow at all costs.

A Word about Growth

Growth for growth's sake is analogous to replacing one of the springs in our model with a stronger spring. The result is that a larger burden has effectively been placed on the company. Management expends organizational and capital resources and also creates an expectation for that much more growth in the future (after all, they did it once). But profitability has suffered just a bit, and because the company has grown, achieving the same growth *rate* in the future requires even larger opportunities. And if the portfolio of opportunities is similar to what was pursued to achieve this growth at all costs, then this pattern will repeat itself. The known portfolio of *profitable opportunities* just became less significant relative to the need for an ever-increasing number of larger and larger opportunities needed for the sake of growth.

Typically, for a sizeable company, the full impact of this year's investments won't be realized until some point in the future, so management can "kick the can down the road" a bit without the impact of these decisions being noticed in the short term. They were able to show the world their ability to grow the company... this time anyway. However, in reality, this pattern cannot be sustained. Pushing for growth at the expense of profitability and repeatability over and over will deplete the company's resources, putting an ever-increasing strain on the firm.

This kind of scenario goes on in companies from all industries throughout the market. We see it over and over. In extreme cases, it can result in a situation like some of the scandals we are all familiar with: Enron, Tyco, and countless others. The pressure to grow is incessant. This pursuit, more than perhaps any other, gets a company into trouble. The consequence of a myopic focus on growth is one of the key lessons of a balanced business model. A company's growth has a natural "speed limit," and exceeding that speed limit results in weakening rather than strengthening the company over time.

Given these discussions about growth, one might ask, "What about so-called 'shrink-to-grow' strategies?" Shrink to grow is actually an excellent example of a company trying to achieve better balance and therefore is, in fact, a balancing activity. Why? Because when a company considers "shrinking," it will often do so by discontinuing or divesting operations which, in their view, are becoming less profitable or are consuming too many resources to sustain alongside other opportunities. The company then chooses to re-focus its efforts. In doing so, it makes a strategic adjustment that effectively causes negative growth, but also results in improved profitability and sustainability. This further illustrates how the three balanced focus areas are interlinked, in tension, and that making any major decision about one actually affects all three.

What kind of growth is most desirable? The short answer is that desirable growth is a relative concept, meaning that the pace of growth desirable for a given company depends upon a number of inherent characteristics of the company itself as well as external factors. Examples of these (among many others) are:

- Inherent characteristics
  - Current scale within its chosen markets
  - Current resources
  - Constraints
- External factors

o   Available opportunities

o   Peer performance

o   Market expectations

So desirable growth is complicated. However, desirable growth for all intents and purposes boils down to balanced growth. One of the key insights obtained by conceptualizing a company's three broad objectives or areas of focus being in tension is the importance of balanced growth. We believe that the most desirable growth is profitable growth – that is sustainable over multiple business cycles. We cannot overemphasize how important it is to think of it in such simple terms. The problem is that profitable growth must be achieved in the face of multiple constraints – broadly, these are financial, market, and execution constraints. We believe that a business model which enables balanced growth allows for optimal use of precious resources of all types and leads to greater value creation for shareholders over time.

Considering the complicated nature of growth, the use of appropriately detailed financial modeling is often required to see the overall impact of various growth scenarios and to ensure that relevant constraints are considered. The kind of financial model we're talking about is not the relatively simple model you might build in an MBA finance class or even what a Wall Street analyst might create. Rather, it is a key business driver-based model which enables the company to make real decisions about multiple areas of its portfolio. It is more akin to a simulation of the company's future – a simulation that can help answer questions such as:

- Should we [add a new production line or expand capacity]?
- Should we consider divesting [this business unit]?
- What is the impact of our latest market outlook, and what if conditions are better or worse than expected?
- Under what conditions does further investment in [this area] make sense within the larger portfolio?

- When does the hopper of known future opportunities run dry?
- Do we have the financial capacity to proceed with this plan, or will we break debt covenants?
- At what point will we have to make major changes to our capital structure?
- Etc.

The visual of the spring framework is an ever-present mental reminder of the effects of undue focus or action in any one area. But this so-far purely conceptual framework can be taken further. One of the authors has developed a way to apply this framework to obtain valuable insights about a company's ability to achieve profitable, sustainable growth and therefore benchmark the sustainability of its business model. This process involves choosing appropriate metrics to represent each of the three focus areas (growth, repeatability, and profitability). The idea is to gather metrics on each of the three factors for an appropriate group of peer companies and numerically represent these objectives or areas of focus within the balanced business model framework. When an industry or group of peers is analyzed in this way, the ultimate metrics calculated for plotting are entirely relative to what was achieved by each of the peers in the group. (This, of course, makes choosing an appropriate set of peers quite important.)

Consider for a moment whether this makes sense: If I want to have some idea about whether my growth or profitability is satisfactory and reasonably appropriate, I may want to compare how my results stack up to that of my peer group. The section that follows illustrates the outcome of just such an exercise, including an illuminating example of one company with a demonstrable ability to consistently operate in a balanced business model manner. The value of such an exercise is this: Companies which operate in a demonstrably balanced manner are relatively few. So when an example of such a company is discovered, it may be worth examining that company's business model and strategy in some depth, asking yourself questions such as:

- What is this company's business model, and how is it different from others' in the group?
- What do they do differently than we do? What do they do more of? What do they do less of?
- What enables this company to achieve consistently balanced results?
- How is their business model manifest in their operating and financial metrics?
- What prevents [my company] from achieving similarly consistent, balanced results?
- What are they doing that we have not been willing to do, but which we could change?

Having a base knowledge of and understanding the differences between each company in the group will be key to asking and answering the right questions. The relative differences in each company which explain the results then become examples of what the result might be of your company pursuing a changed strategy. In the next section, we will examine the results of a peer group of companies from the oil and gas industry which we analyzed by applying the balanced business model objectives framework.

An Industry Analyzed from a Balanced Business Model Perspective

Having now discussed some underlying balanced business model concepts, we can turn our attention to some real-world company analysis. The analyzed companies come from the Oil and Gas industry – E&P (Exploration and Production) companies. Going into detail about how the analysis is performed is beyond the scope of this book. We'll stick to a brief explanation. First, we chose three metrics, each being representative of one of the broad balanced business model objectives. The metric chosen to represent growth was the three-year percentage growth in *output* (production rate), and a *return* metric was chosen to represent profitability. These metrics are generic and analogous enough to apply generally to almost any company.

Of the three objectives, the repeatability (or sustainability) element is the most difficult for which to define an immediately appropriate metric. However, an objective and useful metric in the petroleum industry can represent this parameter. It is called the *reserve life* or *R-to-P ratio*. Very simply, the reserve life represents the total volume of proved oil and gas reserves at the end of a year, divided by the total oil and gas produced within that year. The calculation yields a number that can be interpreted to show how many years of proved reserves a company has. Clearly, this is an E&P-focused metric, and appropriate metrics would need to be identified for any given industry to be so analyzed.

The data set included fourteen E&P companies. For illustrative purposes, we'll show only four companies, even though ten years of data (from 2001 to 2010) for all fourteen companies were used to perform the actual analysis.

While much more can be gleaned from the analysis given more time, our goal for now is to observe how the Objectives in Tension graph of a given company appears over time when compared with the exact same metrics for its competitors.

Business Model Balance Strategies over Time with Data from Four E&P Companies

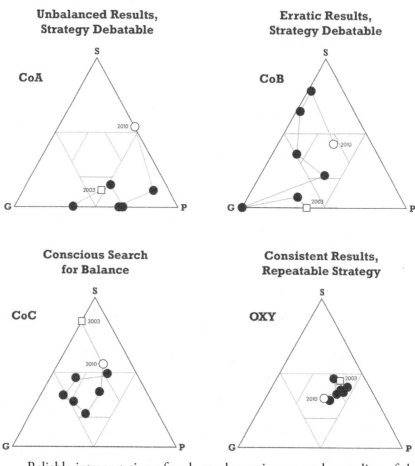

Reliable interpretation of each graph requires an understanding of the underlying data, the methodology, and realizing that each of the data points is relative. They are relative in that a single point's position on the graph is only determined by the results of all three metrics for the company relative to the results of all the other companies in the analysis. Our intent is not to provide a detailed analysis. Rather, we focus on how each graph looks relative to the others and in comparison to the descriptive headlines shown above each company's graph. Having said that, let's dive into commentary of each graph.

In each of the graphs, the open circle indicates the first year, and the open square indicates the last year. In reading the graphs, note that if a point lands on one of the lines of the triangle, this means that a company was *the worst* relative to its peers in the objective indicated by the vertex opposite the line. This will become clearer as we discuss the first company.

Looking at Company A (upper left graph), we see that its data skewed away from repeatability, indicating that this was a weakness for this company. It started off relatively balanced between growth and profitability, but based on this data, we would predict that at some point problems would arise as the company could not sustain its performance forever without strengthening its portfolio. In fact, four of the eight data points for Company A were on the line opposite the repeatability vertex, giving Company A the weakest score for this metric out of all the analyzed peers for fully half of the analysis. By the seventh year, we see that the company's results begin to skew even more, specifically, toward the profitability vertex, which means a second weakness formed – in this case, a dramatic decrease in growth. By the final year of data, sustainability improved, no doubt, due to its worst-in-class growth. In summary, Company A was unbalanced. It was able to pursue profitable growth for six of the eight data points, but eventually its growth became the worst of its peers. If the market liked this company only because of its growth, we would expect a dramatic decrease in value relative to its peers when this reversed.

Company B started off skewed. It had worst-in-class repeatability, and two years later, it had *only* growth going for it, though even that could be weak. We don't know for sure by looking at the graph alone, but our experience leads to some conclusions here. When a company is in or close to one of the corners, almost everything is weak. It takes only a slight imbalance to skew it to one of the corners. A point in a corner means a point that is on two lines. The reader will recall that if a point is on a line, it had worst-in-class performance in the objective opposite the line. So if a point is on a corner, the company had worst in class performance in *two* metrics. From this perspective, Company B is not doing well, being worst-in-class in both repeatability and profitability. At that point in time, the company had no visibly sustainable profits *relative to its peers*. So it gets to work trying to correct these things, no doubt by cutting expenses, and it moves dramatically toward the center. But profits appear to be elusive, and it now moves toward the sustainability vertex, away from both growth and profit. Finally at the very end, the company seems to be moving in the right direction.

Company C begins the journey with a problem: weak and unprofitable growth. But it makes moves in the right direction and is seeking balance. It circles around the center of the triangle, admirably making course corrections, though it appears to be in danger of heading back to where it started. Such seeming conscious movement in a circle around the center suggests management has some idea of what it needs to be doing in the long run, but it just hasn't systematized everything yet to where they can be more consistent.

The most dramatic point demonstrated by the above graphs is the amazingly balanced consistency of *just one* of the companies. That company is Occidental Petroleum (ticker: OXY).

E&P Returns Compared with the ARCA Oil & Gas Index

Over the ten-year time period covered by the data, Occidental Petroleum's stock appreciated almost ten-fold. Over this same period of time, the NYSE ARCA Oil & Gas Index appreciated less than two-fold, as seen in the graph below. To be fair, the ARCA Oil & Gas Index includes supermajors, state-owned oil companies, refiners, and larger E&Ps (including

OXY and five more companies included in our 14-company data set), so it is quite a broad index. With this in mind, the Total Shareholder Return (TSR) graph below also shows the returns of three other companies we chose to highlight in our ternary diagrams above.

The returns make sense relative to the story told in the ternary diagrams or objectives in tension analysis. Company A seems to be knocking it out of the park until the financial crisis – its share performance being almost as strong as OXY. But it must have been stretching its resources thin – no doubt financial resources – and it never recovers after the financial crisis. It wasn't operating in a sustainable manner. In the last few years, its value erodes dramatically, and it is the only one of the four that doesn't come close to returning to its value before the recession.

Company B, as our balanced objectives analysis supports, starts off weakly. In fact, it begins with negative returns in the first few years. Over the entire period, it shows the weakest returns. In the very last year, it seems to have found its way a bit. Its share price declines less in mid-2010 than the others, and finally in the last third of the year, it begins to appreciate at a rate higher than all but OXY. It also delivers returns that beat the index in the last year.

Company C also starts off weak. Its returns, like Company B, are negative in the beginning. But it continues to improve. Eventually it delivers strong returns in the middle of the period and almost recovers its peak value after the financial crisis. In its conscious search for balance, it eventually delivered significant value to shareholders, outsized returns relative to the index in the last few years.

The total shareholder returns graph shows that all four of these companies, as well as the index, at least tripled in value from 2001 to mid-2008, which was when oil prices hit their all-time peak and just before the financial crisis hit in full force. One of the companies was achieving returns that approached those of OXY up until prices peaked. Then prices collapsed and all were hit dramatically, as was virtually the entire market. But after oil prices ceased their free fall, stabilized, and began to grow, OXY was in a class by itself. OXY had superior returns throughout the entire 10-year period, both before and after the financial crisis.

Consistent Results, Repeatable Strategy

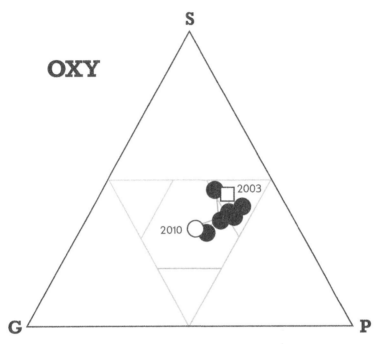

If we examine OXY's diagram, we see impressive consistency of balance – its results clustered very tightly in the chart. But we also note one other characteristic. Of the three objectives, one was relatively weaker for most of the 10-year period. That objective was (production) growth. It was absolutely balanced in being both profitable and being able to deliver repeatable results into the future, but OXY made choices to grow a bit less dramatically than its peers. By the end of the ten-year period, however, OXY's results were almost perfectly balanced, as indicated by the data point for 2010, which rests at dead center of its graph. No doubt, this was due to its ability to pick up where it left off after the economic crisis.

The difficulty of the challenge to an organization's processes, strategy, and leadership of balancing these three factors consistently should not be underestimated. In truth, most organizations remain focused on a single factor such as growth (or profitability) to the detriment of the other two – or may swing unpredictably in one direction or another, depending on what kind of market or financial pressure they are currently reacting to. Our experience suggests that many companies tend to aggressively pursue one of the three factors at the expense of the other two, often in successive years. In today's quarterly results-driven atmosphere, growth is often chased while profitability suffers or vice-versa. It may be necessary to shift markedly toward just one of the three factors in the short run. But from a more strategic point of view, meaning over the longer term of three to six years, attempting to balance growth, profitability, and repeatability will result in a more successful business model.

Constraints to Business Model Balance

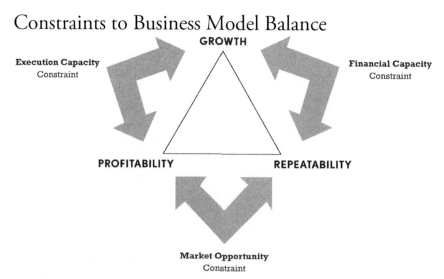

You may find it challenging to balance the objectives of a balanced business model and with good reason. Ever-present constraints limit the three fundamental objectives of growth, profitability, and repeatability. These constraints represent countervailing forces that make it difficult to balance the company's business model, even when you are aware of the need to do so and committed to accomplishing it. The three constraints are:

- Market Opportunities
- Execution Capacity
- Financial Capacity

Market Opportunities

In order to grow year after year a company needs to identify an adequate number of *Market Opportunities* of sufficient magnitude to make a meaningful difference in its annual revenue stream. Whether the number of opportunities is too little – or the size of those opportunities (relative to the current revenue base) is too small – doesn't make much difference. The company will be challenged to grow at satisfactory levels. Company executives frequently overlook the supply of sufficiently meaningful opportunities going forward over the next two to three years. When modeling future growth, you need to know *specifically* which opportunities you are planning for. You also need to know the magnitude and profitability of each opportunity in terms of revenue, impact on the company, and so on. The view and assumptions about market opportunity should be supported by objective analysis that is informed by the common fact base we discussed earlier.

Execution Capacity

Similarly, in order to manage costs and increase profitability year after year, the company must have the focus, resources, and skills to execute on its strategies and optimize its business processes. This *Execution Capacity* often separates winners from losers in the marketplace and limits the ability of a firm to perform at desired or expected levels. No matter how modest or ambitious the objectives of the business, the ability to execute will constrain and limit those plans. We will deal extensively with the topic of strategy execution in subsequent chapters.

Financial Capacity

Few if any organizations have unlimited financial resources. Hence, *Financial Capacity* will always be a constraint on the organization's ability to invest for the future. Financial capacity affects each of the key elements of the business model as well as the other two constraints mentioned above. Financial capacity is often the most obvious and dominant of the three constraints we mention here, particularly for new or troubled businesses. The financial capacity we refer to here can mean cash flow, capital availability, credit rating, current and long-term debt ratios, and so on.

Combined Effect of Constraints

We can think of the three issues mentioned above in combination to be constraining growth, profitability, and repeatability in this manner: each of the three constraints has the ability to affect one or all of the elements needed to successfully balance the company's business model. This framework provides a set of checks and balances against which we can test our business plans and models to confirm that our constraints will not undermine our strategies.

Shifting Business Model Balance Impacts Results

Referring to recent shifting business practices by Ford and GM, *The Wall Street Journal* (*WSJ*) reported, "Where the US auto companies once were more focused on sales crowns, pumping out higher volumes at razor-thin margins, they now are flourishing by focusing on what customers want to buy. It is about consistency, said Ford CFO Bob Shanks. While the years since the financial crisis haven't all been milk and honey, Ford, like GM, has chosen to focus on the bottom line, while bigger rivals chase sales crowns."[19]

The concept of improving business model balance in the automotive industry has not been lost on Fuji Heavy Industries, the maker of Subaru automobiles. *WSJ* reports, "One of the industry's little guys is quietly emerging as one of its biggest when it comes to profit margins. The company recently posted 17.5% operating margin for latest quarter, far exceeding larger Japanese auto makers and widely outpacing German luxury brands. 'We want to be an automaker that dominates with profit margins and quality rather than quantity,' says CFO Mitsuro Takahashi."

A more balanced business model seems to be paying off for Subaru. Their ability to focus on profitability, repeatability, and growth simultaneously appears to be driving superior results. *WSJ* points out, "Through June of 2015, its US market share stands at 3.2%, after more than a half-decade of steady increases. Once among the smallest players, Subaru now solidly outsells Mazda, Volkswagen, and Germany's luxury brands, having posted an average annual sales increase of nearly 19% since the US financial crisis."[20]

A balanced business model encompasses the processes, standards, methodologies, capabilities, and markets chosen by the firm. Without all of these elements being in sync in a way that enables simultaneous focus on the three objective outcomes, a company encounters difficulty in its efforts to deliver *value*. Because value creation is key to your long-term success equation, any test or set of metrics which shows a company lacking relative to its competitors in one of the three balanced outcome factors suggests that there may be problems with the company's business model.

Ultimately, the three business model balance factors boil down to the manner in which a company decides to invest and allocate resources. Where and how a company chooses to invest its resources *now* determines its future growth, its repeatability, and its profitability. Unfortunately, with short-term reporting concerns so often dominating the focus of top executives, the longer-term future – the true source of value – is too often at the mercy of this year's (or even this quarter's) results. This is why executives need to be absolutely clear on their priorities – to their employees, to the board, and to the market. Valuation is all about the future, as is investment. Investing in the right way – and in a repeatable, methodical way – is key to sustainable value creation.

Changing an existing business model or shifting the fundamental direction and nature of the business must in turn be reflected in the strategic goals, strategies, and key initiatives of an organization. We discuss formation of these goals, strategies, and initiatives at length in a later chapter.

Chapter 4 – Business Model Assessment
Key Thoughts & Takeaways

Before proceeding to the next chapter, please take a few minutes to think about the following with your organization in mind:

What are my key takeaways from this chapter?

What issues have I observed in my company or organization?

What are the implications for my organization?

5. Vision & Mission Alignment

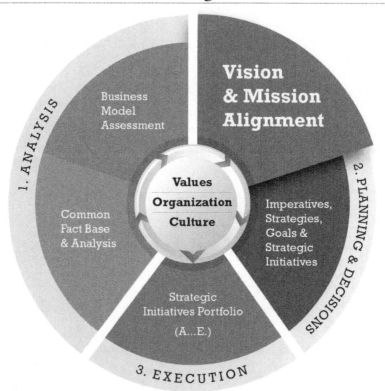

They err in vision, they stumble in judgement. [1]

Vision. Mission. Strategic intent. These phrases have become almost trite in today's management lexicon. It seems every business, division, department, and team has defined one or more of these descriptors to create an identity. Vision-like phrases are so commonplace now as to be seen and used as slogans to differentiate one entity or function from another.

However commonplace vision statements may have become, when viewed through the lens of enterprise-level strategic planning, does it really make sense to formulate a multi-year strategic plan without a statement of purpose and the benefit of an aspirational vision of the future for the business?

Vision, Mission, or Slogan?

How do we differentiate between vision, mission, and other descriptors of business intent? While recognizing the value to organizations of visionary descriptors, companies are still left with a variety of choices about how to express their intentions or direction for the future. Whether in advertisements, on websites, or in communications with shareholders, you will find descriptors ranging from short slogans to well-thought-out statements of vision and purpose. We believe there are essentially four types of descriptors. Here are publicly available examples organized and defined by type. The four types of statements are listed below in the order of increasing strategy definition importance:

1. **Catch Phrase (or Tag Line):** A pithy line or phrase designed to quickly describe who we are, what we do, or something we would like to be known for:

    FedEx: "The world on time"

    General Electric: "Imagination at work"

    Disney World: "The happiest place on earth"

    Greyhound: "Leave the driving to us"

    Gillette: "The best a man can get"

    Hallmark: "When you care enough to send the very best"

2. **Mission Statement:** A longer declaration that communicates primarily what business we are in – and sometimes why. It can describe who we are and what purpose we serve in the world or the market place:

105

Google: "Google's mission is to organize the world's information and make it universally accessible and useful."[2]

Dwolla (mobile payment company startup): "Allow Anything Connected to the Internet to Move Money Quickly, Safely, and at a Cost as Low as Possible."[3]

Merck & Company: "To discover, develop and provide innovative products and services that save and improve lives around the world."

Boeing: "People working together as a global enterprise for aerospace leadership."

3. **Statement of Strategic Intent:** The implied motivations that underlie and explain our strategy which could be short term or longer range. It acknowledges what drives our strategy, whether or not for public consumption.

Canon: "Beat Xerox"

Komatsu: "Encircle Caterpillar"

Honda: "Become a second Ford"

Coca-Cola: "Put a Coke within arm's reach of every consumer in the world"

(For more on "Strategic Intent" see the article by Gary Hamel and C.K. Prahalad in the July 2005 *Harvard Business Review*.)

4. **Vision Statement:** The level of success, reputation, excellence, or accomplishment to which we as an enterprise or business unit wish to aspire and commit ourselves.

WellStar Health System: "The vision of WellStar Health System is to deliver world-class healthcare through our hospitals, physicians and services."[4]

Amazon: "Our vision is to be earth's most customer centric company; to build a place where people can come to find and discover anything they might want to buy online."[5]

General Electric: "We have a relentless drive to invent things that matter: innovations that build, power, move and help cure the world. We make things that very few in the world can, but that everyone needs. This is a source of pride. To our employees and customers, it defines GE."[6]

Merck & Company: "To make a difference in the lives of people globally through our innovative medicines, vaccines, biologic therapies, consumer care and animal health products. We aspire to be the best healthcare company in the world and are dedicated to providing leading innovations and solutions for tomorrow."[7]

Alibaba's Aspiration for China: Alibaba's aim is simple and ambitious. It is, as Jack Ma (Alibaba's founder and executive chairman) puts it, "to be the infrastructure of commerce in China." Its focus is on small businesses, helping them to sell through its Taobao marketplace, providing financial services through Alipay, and offering logistical support through its cloud computing and data platform.

From the several descriptive examples and four categories above, clearly, you can describe a business in multiple ways – its purpose and its direction. Business leaders may want to apply some or all of these "word vehicles" to communicate direction and strategy in ways that are most appropriate for their organization within its current environment. For purposes of strategic planning, we suggest a current, well-defined, broadly supported, and communicated enterprise-level vision statement. Alignment of the organization's vision and strategies is a critical factor for successful strategy development and execution.

Enterprise level vision statements are more valuable to the organization when they meet all or most of the following criteria. A good Vision statement is:

1. **Developed Collaboratively** – i.e., not the vision of a single executive
2. **Supported by the Entire Executive Team**
3. **Aspirational** – stating who or what we intend to become, not just what or who we are
4. **Motivating** – credible and meaningful to all; people are readily willing to sign up to help achieve the vision
5. **Stretching to the Organization** – not something we have already achieved; vision will push us to a new level of achievement or performance
6. **Short and Succinct** – meaning a paragraph or two
7. **Written in the Present Tense** ("we are" rather than "we will be")
8. **Consistent with the firm's business model and its future direction**

More broadly speaking, then, a vision statement becomes a useful tool depending upon a) the way it comes to be, b) the meaning it holds for stakeholders, and c) the language it employs.

If a vision statement already exists for the business, we suggest that representatives of the various departments and levels in the organization be asked to comment on the existing vision in light of the eight criteria above. If the vision statement does not fare well against these eight criteria – or when compared for consistency with business model direction and plans – it may be necessary to revise or replace it. And in order to address and meet the above criteria, while defining a new vision, we suggest asking these questions before attempting to move forward with vision statement creation or revision:

1. Do we have (or need) a vision for the future?
2. Do we understand the difference between a vision, a mission, or a statement of strategic intent?

3. How far forward should a vision take us?
4. How do we go about defining it?
5. Who should be involved in articulating it?
6. How do we communicate it?
7. How do we gain acceptance and support for our vision?
8. Can we successfully plan in the absence of such a vision?
9. Whose vision should it be?
10. How do we become aligned as a leadership team around our vision?
11. How do we reconcile department or business unit vision statements with our enterprise vision?

Creating an "Inspiring Vision for the Future"

In the pragmatic approach to strategic planning, we make the assumption that strategies, goals, and initiatives are defined and planned in the context of an overarching strategic vision for the future of the business. Since strategic decisions more often than not represent multi-year investments and commitments, it is critical that these decisions are not only consistent with, but enabling of the long-term character, vision, and intent of the organization. A vision is sometimes referred to as "a word picture of our preferred future." Such an inspiring vision describing the company's intended future is most important to two audiences in particular:

- Customers – who need to know what the aspirations and future direction are of the business they are dealing with
- Managers and employees at all levels – who need to understand and support at a personal level where their company is headed in the future

Of course this same knowledge and understanding of the enterprise vision is certainly beneficial for all the firm's business partners, suppliers, creditors, and the like. But in our view, these other entities do not feel the impact to the same extent as customers and employees.

Having a vision statement (at almost any level, department, division, and so on) has become commonplace in recent times. It seems fashionable and almost obligatory to have one. Since not having a vision seems unacceptable, the important thing to some leaders may be to simply make sure the box has been checked.

The vision for the entire *enterprise*, however, is of far greater consequence than any other that does or could exist in the firm. The enterprise vision should be the umbrella under which all other vision statements in the organization fall and with which they should also be conceptually and directionally consistent.

Sometimes we need only look to non-profit or charitable organizations to find examples of an inspiring mission or vision. A case in point is the vision of the Cure Alzheimer's Fund. Their mission is to: "Fund research with the highest probability of preventing, slowing or reversing Alzheimer's disease." Their strategy, which contains elements of both vision and business model states:

"A venture capital approach to medical research by finding the visionaries in the field, supporting them, focusing on the essentials by establishing a frugal culture and daring to be great."[10]

The Cure Alzheimer's Fund is one of the most highly rated charitable funds in America according to Charity Navigator, an organization that evaluates and rates charitable organizations. An indication that Cure Alzheimer's Fund is living up to its vision is that Charity Navigator gives it a 99.07 (out of a possible 100) score based on financial performance, accountability, and transparency.

One of the key reasons for the fund's high rating is that donors' money goes directly into cutting-edge research that is performed by a scientific team at Harvard and about twenty-five other institutions. Those familiar with the fund say it's unique as a philanthropy because its founders and board members pay for all overhead and operating expenses. Among the fund's most significant breakthroughs is "Alzheimer's in a Dish" where researchers grew human brain cells in a petri dish and gave the cells genes for the disease so they could observe how the disease progresses and how drugs can treat it.

We would expect a non-profit to have a clear and lofty mission that easily translates to a vision or mission statement. Unfortunately, many executives in for-profit organizations are a bit flummoxed when faced with the need to create an appropriate and inspiring vision for their organization. So just how do executives go about developing an effective vision statement that meets the criteria we have discussed?

When developing a more advanced digital strategy, the best approach may be to turn the traditional strategy development process on its head. Benn Konsynski, the George S. Craft Distinguished University Professor of Information Systems & Operations Management at Emory University's Goizueta Business School, proposes that rather than analyzing current capabilities and then plotting an organization's next steps, organizations should work backwards from a future vision.

"The future is best seen with a running start," Konsynski comments. "Ten years ago, we would not have predicted some of the revolutions in social media or analytics by looking at these technologies as they existed at the time. I would rather start by rethinking business and commerce and then work backwards. New capabilities make new solutions possible, and needed solutions stimulate demand for new capabilities."[11]

The visioning process can actually be quite straight forward. We have helped numerous organizations develop vision statements that meet the criteria just introduced. But before discussing the process, we want to note that, vision creation can be difficult to achieve or even attempt in a large group setting. Little meaningful work is accomplished in groups of more than ten people. Developing a meaningful, well-supported vision statement is best accomplished using a capable person to help facilitate the process with the participating executives. Without facilitation, the most senior voice dominates, and fewer voices are heard.

You can add value by articulating purpose and direction using any of these four descriptive vehicles:

- Catch Phrase or Tag Line
- Mission Statement
- Strategic Intent Statement
- Enterprise Vision Statement

However, for purposes of strategic planning, we believe that an enterprise vision statement is the more valuable because of its ability to define the future direction on the business, inspire its people, and especially create alignment among a team of executives – when they are directly involved in defining such a vision. Other expressions of organizational focus or purpose should be highly consistent with the organization's enterprise vision, whether they apply to the organization as a whole or focus on subsets of the overall business. For these reasons, we now turn our attention to a pragmatic process by which a team of executives can collaborate to efficiently create a shared vision.

How Do You Create an Inspiring Vision for the Future?

An effective vision should reflect the purpose and "soul" of an organization, but must also be succinct and inspiring. So how do you go about doing this? In short, you ensure that it reflects the thoughts and aspirations of the executive team. To systematically ensure this, we suggest a step-by-step process designed to help a group of executives collaboratively develop and agree on a vision statement. The following steps walk you systematically through this process:

1. Bring the executives together in a neutral setting or conference room to work together on the vision.

2. Describe the purpose and agenda for the meeting. Acknowledge that this is a working session and that enterprise vision creation is the goal for the meeting and that this session may or may not result in a final version of the vision

3. Ask each executive to individually and privately write down several key words or phrases that they believe should be included in the company's vision. (Alternatively, executives can be surveyed in advance to gather the key words or phrases to be introduced in step four.)

4. Ask each executive to then write their preferred words and phrases on a flip chart or white board.

5. Give the executives a few minutes to look at and review all the words and phrases that have been so posted.

6. Ask each executive individually to present to the rest of the group his or her key words and phrases – stating why these particular word or phrases were chosen.

7. Allow each member of the group to then respond to the presenter about which words or phrases are most attracting or positive for themselves – and why

8. After all have presented their preferred words and phrases, break the group into small groups of two to four people and ask them to create a draft vision (of no more than two paragraphs) using the words and phrases that were presented and discussed in steps three through seven.

9. Ask each small group to write their proposed vision on a flipchart or whiteboard.

10. Ask each small group to present their draft vision statement to the entire group.

11. After a draft vision has been presented, open discussion to the entire group and ask for comments about which phrases or elements attract them to the draft vision and which phrases or elements do not – and why.

12. After the draft vision statements have been presented and discussed, ask one or two people from each small group to work together to write a second draft of the vision statement – *combining the best thoughts and phrasing from the initial draft visions.*

13. Ask the group that has combined the earlier drafts into a second draft to present the combined vision draft to the entire group.

14. Allow each member of the entire group to state what appeals to them or attracts them to the vision – or does not.

15. Revise or tweak the vision statement as appropriate based on comments from the group.

16. Test the group for degree of alignment and consensus on the now revised vision statement.

17. Ask the most senior executive to comment on his or her feelings about the vision.

18. Decide whether the vision is sufficiently aspirational and motivational to adopt as stated or whether the vision needs additional work or some wordsmithing. Assign next steps or schedule another meeting to finalize the vision.

19. Discuss how and when the vision should be shared with others in the organization.

20. Document all final wording and decisions.

While this process for vision creation may seem long and complicated, we have found that it can typically be done with a group of senior leaders in a few hours of dedicated effort – think in terms of a half-day. The visioning process is designed to achieve four important objectives:

1. Create an inspiring, purposeful vision for the future.
2. Achieve alignment among participating executives around the vision that has been written.
3. Prepare us for communicating the vision to others.
4. Set the stage for strategic decision making and planning.

As you begin articulating the vision, remember that:

- The vision for the business is closely connected to its values and culture. If company culture is a source of strength or pride, the vision should reflect that culture. Alternatively, the culture may be influenced and shaped by the vision. As the vision gains acceptance, less-than-desirable cultural elements may be changed over time.

- The visioning process will yield meaningful and lasting results if developed within the proper context. The visioning step purposely occurs after the analysis activities which produce a common fact base, assessment of the business model, and high-level strategic imperatives. In absence of this context, the process can devolve into producing inspirational, but unfounded goals.

Lou Holtz, the former and still famous Notre Dame football coach, said, "You have to have a vision of where you want to go. Without a vision you have nothing. You have to have a plan of how you're going to get there. And you have to lead by example."[11]

In the next chapter, we examine the role that the organization's values, culture, and structure play in vision, strategy formulation, and execution.

Chapter 5 – Vision & Mission Alignment
Key Thoughts & Takeaways

Before proceeding to the next chapter, please take a few minutes to think about the following with your organization in mind:

What are my key takeaways from this chapter?

What issues have I observed in my company or organization?

What are the implications for my organization?

6. Values, Culture, & Organization

Culture eats strategy for breakfast!
– Peter Drucker

Earlier we stated, "Strategic planning is always done in the context and *under the influence of the organization's values, culture, and structure.* Naturally, the plan inevitably reflects these. In some organizations, values and culture need to be addressed or perhaps even re-defined to put a strategic plan in place that is authentic from a values and culture perspective." In others, the organization's culture and values are already firmly in place.

Although it may seem an interruption to consider Values, Organization Structure, and Culture when we have progressed through only three of the five elements of the pragmatic strategic planning model, we actually view it as somewhat irresponsible to move beyond vision and mission alignment without beginning to address these three intangible areas. Values and Culture in particular will impact the strategy of the business – and perhaps even more so, its ability to execute that strategy.

Organization Culture & Values

Speaking on the topic of corporate culture, Apple's CEO Tim Cook said, "The culture of a company to me defines how excellent it will be, how innovative it will be. But if there's self-honesty in the culture, it also defines how quick it is to admit the mistakes that every company makes. There's a whole set of things. Does a company have integrity or not? Does a company desire to do something more important than simply making money? Is there a reason for being, and do the employees really get the reason for being? Virtually everyone at Apple knows how deeply the culture of the company is ingrained. And in my mind the company wouldn't nearly be where it is today without that strong culture."[1]

In our earlier discussion of business models, we noted the concept of "moats." When they are wide rather than narrow, moats can serve to protect and buffer a business and its underlying assets from competition. Some of the assets that create such a moat are intangible, like patents, trade secrets, and so on. Unusually strong organization cultures should be included among a company's intangible assets. Strong cultures in turn support positive gains in human capital.

Human capital is growing more valuable in every business. This trend has been going on for decades as ever fewer workers function as simply doers and more become thinkers and creators. According to advisory firm Ocean Tomo, intangible assets – copyrights, brands, goodwill, patents – are largely reflections of human skill and creativity. They are by far the biggest source of business value and are still increasing, having grown from only 17% of S&P 500 market value in 1975 to an impressive 84% in 2015.

One of the more reliable indicators over the years of organizations with unusually positive cultures has been *Fortune* magazine's listing of the "100 Best Companies to Work For." These companies prove that great work places work better. According to Fortune's 100 Best Companies issue for 2015, these 100 best companies outperform other companies as investments. Analysis of the publicly traded firms in the rankings from 1984 through 2009 by Wharton's Alex Edmans found that a portfolio of the 100 best companies exceeded its expected risk-adjusted return by 3.5% a year.[2]

In our experience, relatively few organizations do a good job of defining their culture for internal or external consumption. Among the many reasons for this is the fact that organization cultures often evolve rather than being proactively defined and introduced. It seems that many companies are better at defining rules (written and unwritten) and policies than articulating and adhering to their desired culture and values.

In 2015, Google became for the sixth time the number one company on *Fortune's* list of "100 Best Companies to Work For." Not surprisingly, Google is also a company that has done an exemplary job of proactively articulating its culture and values. Closely associated with Google's mission are the values (or beliefs) of its founders:

These beliefs are referred to as "Ten Things We Know to Be True," and they are still embraced by the founders and Google employees today. The Google Beliefs[3] are:

- **Focus on the user and all else will follow**. – Since the beginning, we've focused on providing the best user experience possible....
- **It's best to do one thing really, really well.** – We do search....

- **Fast is better than slow.** – We know your time is valuable, so when you're seeking an answer on the web you want it right away – and we aim to please.
- **Democracy on the web works.** – Google search works because it relies on the millions of individuals posting links on websites to help determine which other sites offer content of value.
- **You don't need to be at your desk to need an answer.** – The world is increasingly mobile: people want access to information wherever they are, whenever they need it...
- **You can make money without doing evil.**
- **There's always more information out there.** – Once we'd indexed more of the HTML pages on the Internet than any other search service, our engineers turned their attention to information that was not as readily accessible...
- **The need for information crosses all borders.** – Our company was founded in California, but our mission is to facilitate access to information for the entire world, and in every language....
- **You can be serious without a suit.** – Our founders built Google around the idea that work should be challenging, and the challenge should be fun...
- **Great just isn't good enough.** – We see being great at something as a starting point, not an endpoint...

Boeing also articulates its corporate values in a list:

The Boeing Values[4] are:

- **Leadership** – We will be a world-class leader in every aspect of our business...

- **Integrity** – We will always take the high road by practicing the highest ethical standards...
- **Quality** – We will strive for continuous quality improvement in all that we do...
- **Customer Satisfaction** – Satisfied customers are essential to our success...
- **People Working Together** – We recognize our strength and our competitive advantage is – and always will be – people...
- **A Diverse and Involved Team** – We value the skills, strengths and perspectives of our diverse team...
- **Good Corporate Citizenship** – We will provide a safe workplace and protect the environment...
- **Enhancing Shareholder Value** – Our business must produce a profit, and we must generate superior returns...

Yet another set of Values has been articulated by UPS.

UPS – Values: Our Enduring Beliefs[5]

- Integrity – It is the core of who we are and all we do
- Teamwork – Determined people working together can accomplish anything.
- Service – Serving the needs of our customers and communities is central to our success.
- Quality and Efficiency – We remain constructively dissatisfied in our pursuit of excellence.
- Safety – The well-being of our people, business partners, and the public is of utmost importance.
- Sustainability – Long-term prosperity requires our continued commitment to environmental stewardship and social responsibility.

- Innovation – Creativity and change are essential to growth.

Many organizations experience disconnects or omissions between values published in the annual report and the values that form the day-to-day culture of the business. UPS, for example, is a highly regimented, hierarchical business where the *unwritten values* of the organization reward (or punish as the case may be) those who follow (or don't follow) orders and honor the chain of command. It may be one of the most military-like businesses in America. We should point out, however, that UPS is also one of the most successful businesses at implementing and measuring the results of its strategic initiatives.

The values and culture of a business are signaled by its key executives – especially the CEO – based on what kinds of behaviors are encouraged, rewarded, or punished in the everyday workings of the culture. Whether those behaviors are encouraged or just tacitly allowed to flourish may be an irrelevant distinction.

We mention culture primarily to offer an explanation as to a possible cause for why some strategic initiatives succeed or fail. They may fail because they are simply antithetical to the culture into which they are introduced. For example, initiatives that require high levels of innovation are often snuffed out in a business where a history and culture of innovation is lacking. Highly innovative people seldom make their careers in organizations that stifle innovation. Noting again the values of Google, one can see why innovation is more likely to take root in their business than in some others.

According to *Fortune*, culture is the way people behave from moment to moment without being told. More employers are seeing the connection from culture and relationships to workplace greatness to business success. Deloitte's latest annual survey of 3,300 executives in 106 countries found that, for the first time, top managers say culture is even more important than leadership.

Four elements of culture that can make the most difference are:

- **Mission** – A larger purpose motivates most of us.
- **Colleagues** – The best people go where the best people are.
- **Trust** - Show people that you consider them trustworthy, and they'll generally prove you right.
- **Caring** – Don't say it, show it.

Google offers an employee benefit it has never publicized: If an employee dies, his or her spouse receives half the employee's salary for a decade. No words could send as clear a message.

Pontoon Solutions, a Florida-based workforce consulting firm, describes their culture in two ways: "our culture" and "our voice."

Our Culture:

Open: We are direct and honest. We say what we do and do what we say. Transparent about everything we do, we always behave with the highest level of integrity towards our customers, partners and each other.

Courageous: Empowered to speak our minds and unafraid of challenging ourselves. We're confident in our creativity and determined to excel.

Dedicated: We emotionally invest in our work and our clients' business to create positive impact. We love what we do.

Our Voice:

Calm: Our brand communicates a sense of calm whenever it's presented to the world. Notably reassuring, it comes from our understanding of what our clients need and our vast experience in delivering it.

Confident: Our communications have a straightforward confidence to them. The fact is, we don't speak unless we have something relevant and original to say. We are viewed as authoritative, never arrogant.

Spirited: Our communications are spirited and dynamic, we seek to engage our audience, not patronize them. Always respectful, we like to inject a touch of wit where appropriate.

These descriptors are helpful to both internal and external stakeholders because they describe the behaviors that are espoused by the company. Describing these behaviors makes it more likely that specific elements of the culture are both recognized and honored in the day-to-day activities of the company's people.

Notre Dame football coach, Lou Holzt, speaking on values said: "What holds a country together, what holds a family together, what holds a business together are core values. And core values are something you would not compromise. Our core values were:

- Do the right thing (because it generates trust among the team)
- Do everything to the very best of our ability with the time allotted (including the little things)
- Care about one another (that's what makes a team)"[6]

Organization Structure

Structure conveys many messages in organizations: power, authority, control, budgets, priorities, command, prestige, history, tradition, and so on. Organization structures are often in flux – evolving back and forth between centralization and decentralization. Organization structures are also one of the first things companies typically begin changing when they run into difficult business conditions. Why? Because they have total control over their structure, unlike control over customers, competitors, and economic conditions – also because it makes them appear to be taking action.

In an earlier chapter, we pointed out that "Rather than even considering the possibility that their company's business model may be failing, leaking, becoming less competitive, under attack, or simply outmoded, executives often misread the undoing of a historically successful business model. Instead, they attribute root causes of decline to more mundane problems. They point to things like ... faulty organization structure...."

Organization structure is much less likely to convey messages of strategic intent, vision, business model direction, innovation, strategic goals, and initiatives. While we do not want to focus extensively on organization structure strategies and models, a number of questions might be raised as the preferred strategies of the business emerge from the planning process:

- Does our organization structure and staffing support our evolving business model?
- Is our organization structure and hierarchy conducive to sufficient levels of innovation?
- Do we have enough of the right people facing the customer?
- Do we have the necessary and sufficient skill sets internally to enable execution of our key strategic initiatives?
- Are our technical resources capable of helping us transition to an increasingly *digital* business model?
- Is our structure preventing us from more successful execution of our chosen strategies?
- Do we know who our future leaders are?
- Does our structure enable or hinder our preferred vision, values, and culture?
- How do we compare with competitors in terms of revenue per employee?
- Does our organization structure support or inhibit execution of our key strategies?

- Does our CIO play a significant role in strategy definition and execution?
- Does our workforce represent a competitive advantage? Why or why not?

Reviewing and discussing these questions after the organization's primary strategies and initiatives have been defined lends insight to the probability of success or failure of the initiatives or overall strategy.

A Word on Executive (or Management) Teams

We wrote this book based on an experience-based assumption that strategy in most organizations is formulated or executed by a group or team of managers – whether a small or large one. An early reviewer of a draft of this book asked the question, "What is your assumption about what kind of a team the managers are who might attempt to apply your planning process?" The short answer is that we make no assumption about the characteristics of any management team that attempts to use the pragmatic planning process. The process can be used by a cohesive, team-oriented group of executives or by a more self-interested (or even dysfunctional) group of managers. Anyone with business experience that spans multiple organizations recognizes the reality that there is a broad spectrum of collaborative and team behaviors – which can vary widely from one organization to the next.

In our experience, highly collaborative, cohesive management teams have certain characteristics, including:

- Shared experiences
- Shared challenges
- Shared vision and goals
- Shared values
- Mutual respect and openness
- Shared behavioral norms and integrity

- Shared commitment to excellence and achievement

Executives teams that exhibit these (or similar) characteristics should find the pragmatic planning process comfortable and natural. On the other hand, teams that do not possess such characteristics may experience difficulty following the process and may, in fact, find it challenging to reach consensus with their peers on almost any strategic plan, direction, or decisions.

When used as a roadmap for strategic planning, the pragmatic planning process can be helpful to executive teams in progressing toward some of the characteristics mentioned above. Adherence to the process (such as sharing data, defining the vision, formulating initiatives, and so on) requires executives to interact and agree on a path forward for the organization. While this does not guarantee better teamwork, it certainly encourages and facilitates it. We developed the process by observing and experiencing the issues that exist within dysfunctional teams and coming to hypotheses about the drivers of strategic misalignment. We suggest a path toward helping such teams come to a shared view and agreement on the most important concerns they face and the strategic challenges they need to address. If teams can clearly identify these elements, then even where they disagree as to the best solutions, they would ideally still align on why they are pursuing a needed solution set.

Connecting Values, Culture, & Organization to Your Strategy

Authenticity and consistency between an organization's culture and strategy help both when developing plans and executing strategic actions. We need consistency between what we believe about ourselves, what we say we do, and what we actually do. And there needs to be a mechanism in place to check for these inconsistencies, even at the very top of the organization (CEO). An authoritative, arrogant CEO who doesn't pretend to be otherwise may be less than ideal, but one who believes he is otherwise can be even more detrimental to the organization.

We need to have an accurate understanding of what the organization is capable of – what it has been built to do or evolved to become. We need to know the capacity of the business relative to what needs to be accomplished per our imperatives. And we need to understand any limitations now so that required changes to our skills base and staffing can be effected.

"Self-honesty," as Tim Cook describes it, is one of the most important cultural attributes and is key to a company thriving through introspective evolution, rather than by an unexpected, externally-forced event.

Chapter 6 – Values, Culture, & Organization
Key Thoughts & Takeaways

Before proceeding to the next chapter, please take a few minutes to think about the following with your organization in mind:

What are my key takeaways from this chapter?

What issues have I observed in my company or organization?

What are the implications for my organization?

7. Imperatives, Strategies, & Strategic Goals

A recent recruitment listing for a new Group Director within the Bottling Investment Group at The Coca-Cola Company listed the following Strategic Initiatives: "Bottling Investments Group (BIG) *Vision 2020 Strategic Initiatives* such as Revenue Growth Management, Sales Force Effectiveness, Supply Chain Excellence, Procurement and Spend Analysis, Digital Strategy, Mobility Solutions (RED - Right Execution Daily), and Cold Drink Equipment Optimization."

The Coca-Cola Company several years ago introduced its "Year 2020" Vision and Goals and has continued to support and work toward them since – implying a strategic planning horizon of more than ten years. The fact that these 2020 goal areas are included in hiring specifications years later shows a strong organizational awareness of and commitment to the goals. Coke's lengthy commitment toward these goals is laudable, especially in light of the shrinking horizons for strategic planning we discussed earlier. Also, the Kearney survey mentioned earlier revealed that 85% of the companies operating with longer term horizons (such as a strategy lifespan of five years or more) consider their strategies successful.

Strategies may be formulated annually or less often as the situation and available opportunities dictate. However, there is often a need for both long-term strategies (as illustrated in the Coca-Cola example above) and shorter-term strategies. In today's rapidly changing business environment, executives are wise to review the organization's strategies, goals, and initiatives at least annually. Market shifts, competitive landscape changes, and disruptive technologies may require more frequent analysis and review.

A Pragmatic Process for Defining Strategic Actions

Regardless of the time span you cover in your planning, you will require new strategic actions sooner or later, resulting in the need to develop or revise business strategies. Whenever new strategies are called for, we recommend returning to the common fact base stage of the pragmatic planning model to examine or re-examine the *facts* about the situation. Proceed from there to consider the important *implications* of the facts at hand. Then articulate the strategic *imperatives* or actions that arise from thinking through and discussing the facts and implications. Considering these concepts, how then, do we articulate strategy as an executive team?

From Vital Imperatives Will Emerge Strategies

Earlier, we focused on developing a common fact base which must be shared and used to help executives focus on key areas of the business where strategic focus and action is most required. We illustrated the process of advancing from data collection to attachment of strategic meaning to that data by virtue of posing progressively important questions that in turn lead to logical conclusions about our strategic imperatives.

- **Shared Facts:** What are the relevant, most significant and revealing data or strategic facts we have uncovered?

- **Implications:** What do we believe (and agree) are the major implications (financial or otherwise) of these facts for our business?

- **Imperatives:** What insights have emerged from the facts (and their implications) that *should or must compel us to action?*

It is by recognition and articulation of the organization's most important imperatives that you become prepared and ready to nominate and then define the key strategies that are both necessary and sufficient to shape the future of the business. To be seriously considered for adoption, these strategies should be:

- Specific and clear enough to be understood by those who will be involved in executing them
- Sufficiently powerful or impactful to render a strategic difference to the business
- Realistic enough to be workable
- Inspiring enough to motivate the organization

- Executable within specified time frames

Continuing the pragmatic strategy formulation process by agreeing on and documenting our most important facts and their implications, we are now in a position to ask these *candidate strategy* formation questions:

- **Strategies:** Which strategies and actions are required to address the agreed-on implications (financial or otherwise) for our business?

- **Strategic Goals:** What must be measurably achieved as a result of our chosen strategies in order for them to be considered successful?

- **Strategic Initiatives:** What initiatives or programs must be organized, resourced, and undertaken to execute our strategies and deliver on the strategic goals associated with those strategies?

An Example of Defining & Documenting Strategies

Defining strategies is best done by linking the *facts and imperatives* driving necessity with specific strategies that are designed to address them. Linking the imperatives and strategies in this manner serves to provide an ongoing reminder of the *why* behind the strategy. This also helps the team remember what the original motivating factors or rationale were for the strategy, even months or years later. Such linking further aids in efforts to communicate the strategy, whether internally or externally.

By formulating strategies in a logical, sequential manner, critical associations between the common fact base, major implications of the most critical facts, strategic imperatives, and the strategies themselves can be documented and retained in leaders' memories. The chart that follows illustrates how potential strategies emerge by logically defining and connecting the facts, the why (implications), the need (imperatives), and the actions (strategy):

Common Fact Base (the facts) ➡	Strategic Implications (the why) ➡	Strategic Imperatives (the need) ➡	Candidate Strategy (the action)
1. Sales staff report key customers are defecting	1a) Average account size will decrease 1b) Cost for acquiring new customers will impact profits 1c) Sales staff defection may follow	- It is vital to stop the bleeding of larger clients to prevent increased costs from customer defection - We must quickly repair any damage to our image among our largest customers (related to: current products, customer benefits & service levels	- Rapidly create a preferred customer tier of benefits, including a new online service solution - Fill identified gaps in product line - Restore leading-edge image with preferred customers via personal touch – in-person sales calls which include inquiry into needed product and customer benefits
2. Reasons include: No new online products for key customers in past 18-24 months	2. Stale product line may further contribute to customer dissatisfaction and defection		
3. Competitors' customer service ratings improving while ours are declining	3. Leader reputation, a major marketing asset, at risk		
4. Survey data shows clear decline in perceived customer benefit.	4. Risk of further defection of remaining customers		

An Example of Strategy Statement

Following the above recommended progressive/sequential process for strategy formation an actual *statement of strategy* might read something like this:

Preferred Customer Benefit Tier Strategy

- **Because** ... It is vital to our business to slow the turnover among our larger, more profitable customers and be viewed more often by these customers as a leading edge company...

- **Our Strategy is to** ... Create a new tier of preferred customer services and benefits, including a new, more automated online preferred customer mobile and web applications that will be viewed as leading edge.

We now make a rather bold statement: When a strategy is not grounded in this manner (progressively derived from a combination of fact base, implications, and imperatives), it is more likely to have one or more flaws in its premise – or in the organization's ability to execute against it.

Those at the top of the organization, relying on what they believe to be *superior* vision or insight, can be tempted to make irrationally aspirational goals or to articulate strategies which are later shown to be unworkable, misguided, or focused on the wrong things. When this is the case, the organization will likely experience difficulty understanding exactly what a particular strategy element *really* means, what must be accomplished, or even why that element is part of the strategic plan. In such situations, the organization often struggles with internal strategic alignment and is less clear about what each department must contribute or deliver. The result can be either outright failure of a particular element of the strategy or, at minimum, less than optimal execution.

Periodically, we observe CEOs making highly ambitious or vague strategic statements that are not grounded in supporting facts – or that are demonstrably infeasible. The implicit belief of top executives in some cases seems to be: "If I say it over and over, it will happen." Below, we've noted some examples of such statements heard at multiple companies. For each example, we've cited issues that arose after the CEO's statement.

"We will double [output] in [5] years."

- Ability to do so not illustrated via forecast or other understandable mechanism
- Forecasts include unknown or non-existent, overly-optimistic opportunities
- No demonstrated financial capacity to deliver
- Market view not articulated, supported by data, or quantified

"We will grow organically."

- No clear targets beyond the next year
- No proven source of opportunities that leadership is willing to target
- Stated within the context of a dubious track record and uncertain forward plan

"We will become more efficient as we grow, leveraging greater economies of scale." Likely true, but:

- No stated mechanism for achievement
- No specific targets or predictions and thus, no way to quantify expectations, track progress, or monitor success – because there is:
- No basis for determining where and what level of efficiency improvement is an imperative

"We will plan and invest for the long term" (or for long-term shareholders)

- Investment thesis or other explanation lacking to make clear what this really means, but as phrased, it is akin to a statement of values rather than an element of an articulated strategy

Multiple problems arise from unsupported, vague strategy statements or even with a company saying it will do something without demonstrating *how* it will accomplish it. First, the organization's people do not know what they're expected to deliver and cannot work unitedly toward fulfillment. Second, the organization may believe the stated goal is not achievable, particularly in the case of forecasts consisting of non-existent or overly optimistic opportunities. Third, the market can't understand exactly what you will be doing or may not believe the story is credible, which will lead to sub-par valuations or an eventual day of reckoning.

In general, strategy is about what one will DO in the future in response to beliefs about the business environment and the firm's identified opportunity set. If a company does not state what they will actually be doing, then how can this be viewed as an executable strategy?

In our view, a reliable way to avoid such inconsistencies is to adopt a logical process such as we have described, leading to defined statements of strategy. Each strategy element should be formulated in response to an imperative facing the company, which itself has arisen by examining the fact base, taking a view on the future, and identifying the implications. The various imperatives, considered collectively, should in turn lead to a succinct set of statements about those strategic actions that are most critical to the company. This step-by-step process is the essence of *actionable strategy articulation*.

So how do companies wind up with strategy statements that are vague or unsupported? To some extent, they are due to how strategy development has traditionally been taught or practiced. For example, consider a prominent strategy model widely proffered by a major consulting company called

"Capabilities-Driven Strategy." Read carefully, the model ultimately advocates alignment of a company's capabilities and product or service offerings with its chosen markets and stated direction. It states that a *coherent company* first, chooses a clear direction, second, builds a system of differentiating capabilities, and third, sells products or services that "thrive within that system." It further claims that a company that does so earns a "right to win."

We agree that coherency and alignment are crucial, but we see two problems *in the application of this model.* First, the name of the model suggests to the reader that strategy *arises* or is *derived* from capabilities. At a minimum, the model suggests that capabilities are the *drivers of strategy.* Therefore, the model's concept has been used to *formulate* strategy rather than to help achieve the stated aim of *coherency.* In short, we have seen strategies developed or articulated simply by enumerating the strengths (or capabilities) of the company, followed by creating a list of strategy elements which relate to these strengths.

Strategic "coherency" is a worthwhile objective. However, choosing a strategy based on currently existing capabilities alone is problematic. We previously referenced Blockbuster. They could demonstrate an existing differentiated system of capabilities, services which thrived within that system, all of which were consistent with their chosen direction. But this coherent company's current capabilities-driven strategy ended up putting them out of business. Their strategic direction was wrong because it continued to focus on their *current* capabilities. A powerful executive had an *opinion* about the emerging upstart Netflix, dismissing them outright.

Strategy is about what we will do to evolve in response to a future that is in many ways different from the past. Our actions should be planned in response to our beliefs about that future, which in turn must be validated. Basing strategy on historical or current capabilities alone cannot fully address what will be required to lead or even compete in the future.

At the same time, focusing strategies solely on future customers or capabilities dramatically different than (or at the expense of) current reality can likewise be problematic, particularly when you have not established an appropriate context for those strategies. All executives run the risk of making either of these strategic errors, but a new leader brought in from the outside, attempting to demonstrate leadership, is more likely to make such errors.

The New CEO's Dilemma: Ford vs. JC Penney

An incoming CEO often faces a unique dilemma and may be at risk of starting down a strategic path without first doing the necessary groundwork and sufficiently defining diverse strategic alternatives. Imagine suddenly finding yourself at the head of a public company, and imagine further that you are being brought in from the outside to *right the ship* and make significant changes to the firm's traditional ways of doing business. The employees, the board, and the market are all eagerly waiting to hear what your plan will be to put the company on a more value-creating trajectory. You are an accomplished executive and seem to have had a Midas touch up to now. You've arrived at the point where a public company has asked you to lead them. The last thing you want to do is tell these important stakeholders, "I'll get back to you on my plan." You want to demonstrate your business *bona fides* and portray strong leadership, so you feel obliged to explain your ideas for the path forward early on in order to reassure everyone that you are the right person at the right time for the job.

But the new CEO may be well advised to resist the temptation to set forth a plan too early. Numerous examples have shown that CEOs are rarely willing to contradict themselves once they have made public proclamations about the future direction of their company. If a new CEO prematurely commits to a direction – before developing a plan that has naturally progressed and evolved from specific facts and clearly articulated imperatives – making those early directional statements may prove to be regrettable.

More well-considered statements early on actually should be along the lines of, "I'll get back to you." There are fundamental objectives for any corporation, chief among them is creating value for shareholders. Early statements should focus on the CEO's commitment to delivering value and creating a safe environment for employees to surface issues and share ideas that over time will make the company better. Management consultants know that a key part of their work involves interviewing employees, who often know what the issues are and have ideas (too frequently ignored in the past).

One of the better examples of masterfully walking this tightrope is Allan Mulally, who was brought in to lead Ford in 2006. An article in *Forbes* entitled "Why Allan Mulally is an Innovation CEO for the Record Books" by Sarah Miller Caldicort provides insight into Mulally's approach.

"When Mulally took over as CEO in 2006, Ford was in tough shape....

"The cultural shifts Mulally put in place impacted how Ford's teams were structured, how collaboration was fostered, and how innovation itself ultimately came to flourish under his guidance.... By personally modelling candor and a willingness to openly speak about complex, taboo subjects, Mulally built a safe operating environment for his direct reports.... [he] prepared executives to reimagine the future of Ford."

Mulally could have focused on creating a *brilliant* strategy of his own that focused on solving any number of major problems at Ford. But instead, he chose to first empower his people and challenge them to think differently. According to Caldicort, he even played what she called "war games" with his executives, setting up real-time data sessions during which they devised potential scenarios related to major issues they faced. It was this capability that enabled them to navigate the financial crisis and decline government support.

We contrast Mulally's approach with one taken by Ron Johnson, a former Apple executive who was brought in as CEO of JC Penney Company. He was previously credited with putting the *hip* factor into Target. Johnson came in to change JC Penney's stodgy image and attract new customers. It seemed to make sense that someone so successful with Apple and Target could add great value to JC Penney.

Johnson joined JC Penney in November of 2011. As is often the case when an outsider joins a company as CEO, he began to bring in those whom he trusted from his previous companies and fired many of the existing JC Penny executives.

Two months later, in late January 2012, Johnson announced his transformation plan, which included doing away with periodic sales and instead implementing "everyday low prices" in place of special events, sales, and promotions. The JCP stock price jumped immediately, and JC Penney's market cap was soon 25% higher than it had been prior to the announcement, primarily due to the bold words from a CEO who had done great things at other companies. That was the last time the company would be valued at such levels. Johnson's words alone created apparent value because the market simply *trusted him*.

But today, Johnson's tenure at JC Penney is considered one of the most glaringly unsuccessful in retail history. On April 9, 2013 – just 17 months after Johnson joined the company – *Time* magazine stated: "His plans were bold – too bold, virtually everyone now agrees. Correspondingly, he was removed as CEO not because he came up a little short of the goals set for the company. He was ousted because he failed in spectacular fashion."

Time asserts that he "misread Penney's customers." Did he perhaps fail to develop a valid "fact base" about the JC Penney customer? Even if he didn't believe the customer research no doubt already available to him, he made more grievous errors by not observing customers. Further reducing his chances for success, Johnson put his plan in place all at once – as opposed to opting for a pilot and phased roll-out. He dismissed existing data and then ignored the customer by not testing his ideas to confirm whether they would respond as he expected they would. In his mind, he knew what the customer wanted more than they did. He assumed that Apple's *no sales* pricing strategies would also work with JC Penney customers.

By the time Johnson was removed as CEO the company was worth far less than it was worth before he joined the company. At its low, the stock was worth about 85% less (and at the time of this writing remains worth about 75% less).

Having after-the-fact knowledge of JC Penney's new strategy results, it is easy for us to judge Johnson's moves as unwise and ask, "what was he thinking?!" However, it is the dramatic nature of this strategic failure that makes the answer obvious. This is an extreme example of the risks brought about when a single person puts together a plan that is unsupported by a sound, common fact base and analysis. The result was a failure to identify the implications and imperatives that provide a sound directional foundation. The truth is, such leaps in logic are not uncommon in the corporate world and many companies are no longer in business today because of such strategic missteps. More than two years after the departure of Johnson, JC Penney is still at risk as a business.

The consequences of strategic error are not always so dramatic or readily discernable. This often results in the CEO receiving the benefit of the doubt when such errors occur. But imagine how much value has been lost (or has failed to be created) by companies spinning their wheels on strategies that are directionally wrong.

The examples above, though of general interest, are included because they represent situations we have directly observed and provide evidence of the differing outcomes attributable to differing approaches to strategy formulation.

While at times successful strategies do materialize from *gut instinct*, relying on one's instincts alone may not be the most reliable method of strategy development. We have personally observed that, not infrequently, unsuccessful strategies are *gut based*, requiring *trust* in the *brilliance* or track record of a single individual. Often, these strategies could have been proved unviable by some rather basic analysis of existing data.

Although strategies based on a robust data and analysis can and do become unsuccessful, we view a logical, team-based development method to be more reliable. The logic of these strategies can then be transparently illustrated, being tied to fundamental information and analysis. If the strategy proves unsuccessful, it often only becomes apparent why it is unsuccessful when new information becomes available or when circumstances arise which would have been extremely difficult to foresee. A further benefit of the *pragmatic* method is that it can be effected by a defined, reproducible process which depends less on a single individual's *oracle-like* abilities.

Providing Clarity: Defining Goals for Chosen Strategies

After a set of strategies has been defined and agreed on, the next step is to attach specific goals and objectives to each strategy element. This is the first step toward translating these strategies into executable plans. Furthermore, it should be done prior to forming a team to take action on the strategic initiative.

Rather than debating the appropriate time horizon for strategic business goals, define a set of criteria for goals that are both meaningful and strategic for the organization. This is not to suggest that these *particular* suggested criteria should be replicated, but rather that *your organization's* criteria for strategic goal adoption should be defined before you articulate and adopt your actual goals.

Criteria for Setting Strategic Goals

Strategic goals should ideally meet multiple criteria. Each of our committed goals should:

1. Have a strong champion and be supported as well by all members of the executive team
2. Be capable of making a significant difference to the success of the business and customer-perceived value over our chosen time horizon
3. Advance our competitive position or strengthen our business model
4. Support or achieve specific performance metrics or financial targets vital to the business
5. Represent a significant commitment of resources (people, assets, or financial)
6. Rely on competencies that now exist within our business (or will be acquired) to achieve the goal
7. Specifically address one or more of our competitive threats or weaknesses
8. Be time bound
9. Be considered realistically achievable

Strategic goals can be focused on almost any aspect or area of the business as long as the goals are intended to meet criteria such as those listed above. Therefore, we do not suggest which areas of the business they should involve. We do, however, propose that from these qualified strategic goals will ultimately spring a portfolio of the *vital few* strategic initiatives that will drive the business forward. We dive deeper into those strategic initiatives in the next chapter.

We hasten to add that in today's business environment, close attention should be paid to defining technology-related goals and articulating how you will compete against emerging technologies that may affect your firm's competitive position. Most organizations today have reason to believe that emerging technologies have (or will have) the potential to change their business or even fundamental competitive standings in their industry.

A 2014 *McKinsey Quarterly* article concludes that "digitization is rewriting the rules of competition, with *incumbent companies most at risk of being left behind* and – digital capabilities increasingly will determine which companies create or lose value – as new pressure is created on prices and margins and competitors emerge from unexpected places."[2]

Inc. magazine reports that "Venture Capital funding for so-called on-demand mobile services (in which you use an app to order a real-world service) has recently sky-rocketed." *Inc.* calls it a "funding frenzy," pointing out that, "After Uber grabbed $1.2 billion in June 2014, funding to similar companies hit nearly $700 million during just the third quarter of 2014."[3]

Inc. identified at least ten companies (across industries as unrelated as medical services and home repairs, car repairs, and flower delivery) that are leveraging mobile enablement to make the markets they serve more efficient and customer friendly. Matthew Wong, an analyst at CB Insights, which tracks venture capital investment trends, says, "These startups are capitalizing on trends that aren't going away anytime soon: the proliferation of mobile devices and internet access, the sharing economy, and consumers' desire for on-demand services."

CIO magazine recently featured a company called Agero, which has developed a mobile app that eases stranded motorist anxiety by keeping the motorist informed about the location of their tow truck or service vehicle.

"While waiting, the stranded driver can use the mobile app to track the truck's whereabouts on a map in real time. Agero sends a text message notifying the stranded driver when the service vehicle is 10 minutes away."[4]

Before attempting to set and adopt a strategic goal in any area, we should consider the need to ask and answer several straight-forward questions before the goal is actually adopted:

Why is a strategic goal needed in this area? What are we addressing (or responding to)?

What is the nature of the goal we need to set? Are we clear how it will benefit us?

How will we successfully accomplish it? Do we have the means and the commitment to succeed?

How will we measure it?

Who will sponsor and lead the effort? How will we support and hold them accountable?

When must we start and how long will it take?

The first question posed above (why a strategic goal is necessary) may be the most important to answer to the satisfaction of everyone who will be directly involved. In a study about the effectiveness of reengineering and corporate change efforts done by The Atlanta Consulting Group, the most significant finding was contained in a single line: "*Having a compelling need to change is a better predictor of success than any given methodology chosen to drive the change.*"[5]

In the next chapter, we look at how UPS, in order to meet business-critical performance standards, formed a major strategic initiative that leverages technology to achieve a series of goals to improve shipping operations and simplify training for thousands of employees.

Chapter 7 – Imperatives, Strategies, & Strategic Goals Key Thoughts & Takeaways

Before proceeding to the next chapter, please take a few minutes to think about the following with your organization in mind:

What are my key takeaways from this chapter?

What issues have I observed in my company or organization?

What are the implications for my organization?

8. Strategic Initiatives Portfolio Formation & Management

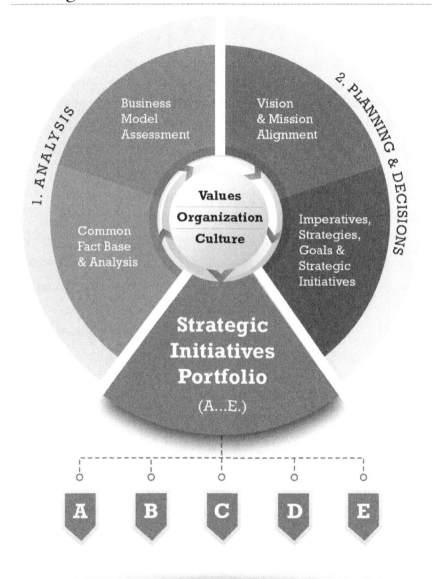

Where the Rubber Meets the Road

Defining and executing the organization's vital few strategic initiatives are the *make-or-break* actions that in the end propel the business in its desired direction and toward its most vital outcomes. One would think that defining without executing or executing without good strategy definition would be rare, but experience tells us otherwise. As an old Welsh proverb warns, "There's many a slip twixt the cup and the lip."

According to General Stanley McChrystal, "The biggest problem is that an organization can get the strategy right, but then can't execute it." Retired General McChrystal was commander of U.S. and International Forces in Afghanistan. He is the founder of McChrystal Group and teaches leadership at Yale University. Gen. McChrystal was interviewed by *The Wall Street Journal* on some of the lessons he has learned in leadership.[1]

According to McChrystal, "There are problems with decision making: People will meet and then not make a decision or they will make a decision and then it won't be implemented. So it's the execution of the organization. And while that seems mechanical, it's really an art. You can't do checklists and make that (decisions) work. It's relationships and the processes you set up that make an organization effective."

As Joint Special Operations Command, General McChrystal recognized that he did not always have the right expertise to make critical decisions and found himself increasingly functioning as "a sort of ringmaster for constant conversation across the command. His contribution was creating the ecosystem where different parts of the organization spoke with each other."

Earlier, we referenced strategic planning research that reported data on 800 executives. The research showed that only 45% of these executives were satisfied with the strategic planning process. Only 23% indicated that major strategic decisions were made within the process of strategic planning. And more than 25% said their companies had plans, but no execution path. This research appears to support the comments of Gen. McChrystal – as well as our experience.

Translating strategies into action (or defining practical actionable strategies) is an element of the strategic planning process that appears to elude or at least challenge many organizations. When the strategic plan for a business or division is a book of ideas put together by a professional planner rather than a course of action decided on by a committed executive team, execution issues will almost certainly follow.

The mechanism by which strategic vision, decisions, and goals can be made actionable and realizable requires defining a carefully selected *Portfolio* of Strategic Initiatives.

Strategic Initiatives Defined

Strategic initiatives are those planned actions, which when taken in concert and properly executed, have the ability to change the arc of an organization's performance, moving it in a desired way toward its strategic objectives, goals, and outcomes.

Strategic initiatives should naturally flow from and exist in support of the vision, goals, and strategic objectives of the business. In a real sense, they are the strategic *bets* the business and its executives make on *how* they will arrive at a more successful condition within a proscribed period of time. These initiatives represent major commitments for the future. In most organizations, we see a range of opportunities and needs. One or two strategic initiatives may be too few and more than six or eight may well be too many.

We use the term "portfolio" to convey the notion of strategic initiatives existing as a mere handful of vital strategic actions or *big bets* which the organization intends to undertake and commit itself to. Such actions often require a year or more, depending on the urgency, scope, complexity, or difficulty of the initiative.

In recent years, analysts have roundly criticized Cisco Systems for choosing to pursue too many key initiatives simultaneously. Cisco has focused on identifying opportunities that represent logical *adjacencies* to its existing business and products to pursue or incubate – in addition to any potential acquisitions it may be considering. They also carefully watched the technology market for inflection points such as the Internet of Things (IoT) to signal where they may want to invest or create strategic initiatives. They then created strategic execution teams for these initiatives. Cisco Systems is not a company of business divisions. That is to say, they do not have separate business units that do very disparate things. In spite of this, it was not uncommon for Cisco to have more than thirty strategic initiatives in progress at one time. This forced initiative teams to compete for resources and management attention in the Cisco environment. In response to analyst criticisms and the difficulty of sustaining so many strategic initiatives at once (not to mention the impact of analyst criticism on its stock price), Cisco has since significantly reduced the number of initiatives being defined and funded. The stock price has rebounded as well.

Identifying Strategic Initiatives

Having educated large corporate major account teams in strategic planning concepts (to better identify issues of key importance and value to their customers), we are often asked, "How can you know whether actions a client is taking are in service of their key initiatives?" We look for several characteristics as signals of real strategic initiatives.

Strategic Initiatives can be recognized when activities or projects related to them meet several or all of the following criteria:

- Set out to change the business or its processes in a major way
- Are related to developing or implementing breakthrough technologies

- Have the potential to improve the organization's business model
- Are considered one of the key forward-looking activities the business is committed to
- Are sponsored by a top executive
- Are led by a senior executive
- Have a significant approved budget
- Have a formal project manager and team
- Are supported and guided by a steering committee
- Have specified numerical or financial goals and objectives to be achieved
- Have a proscribed timeline (with milestone dates and tasks)
- Represent a significant investment for the business
- The cost of failure of the initiative to the business (in terms of dollars or reputation) is high
- Are spinning off multiple sub-initiatives or project teams
- Are attracting or utilizing some of the organization's best people

Not all of these characteristics or criteria need be satisfied in order for an initiative to be considered of strategic importance. Some elements may be lacking and yet the initiative still may be viewed as strategic. If it is truly strategic, however, many if not most of the above characteristics will likely be present.

Lou Gerstner, then IBM CEO, stated in 1973, "...the fact remains that in the large majority of companies corporate planning tends to be an academic, ill-defined activity with little or no bottom-line impact. This lack of real payoff is almost always the result of one fundamental weakness, namely, the failure to bring strategic planning down to current decisions."[2]

It is by means of an intentionally limited, carefully considered Portfolio of Strategic Initiatives that strategic plans merge with and add value to current decisions and today's financial realities. This is where the *rubber* of today business realities meets the *road* to the future of a business. Strategic initiatives are where real-time, team execution of the strategic plan's key elements takes place.

Strategic Initiatives become urgently needed for a variety of reasons, but most typically are formed in response to either threats or opportunities such as:

1. Business problems or shortfalls that are consequential to the health or reputation of the business.
2. Technology advances that represent a threat to harm the business and its market position.
3. Changing regulations or laws that require the organization to change to achieve compliance.
4. Technology advances that represent an opportunity to significantly enhance the business or secure advantage over the competition.
5. Significant or unexpected market share loss.
6. Declining profitability or shrinking margins.

United Parcel Service – Strategic Initiative Needed!

To provide a real-world example of a vitally important strategic initiative, we point to a business-critical situation experienced by the package transport and delivery giant, United Parcel Service (UPS).

During its 2013 peak Christmas holiday delivery period, UPS and its key competitor FedEx both experienced unusual lapses and delays in on-time package pickup and delivery to their Christmas customers. After the dust had cleared and the holidays were over, *The Wall Street Journal* reported that FedEx had delivered 90% of its shipments on time, while UPS deliveries were at just 83%!

For a company that normally delivers better than 99% of packages on time, the 83% performance was both painful and embarrassing for UPS. They were caught off guard when their shipments jumped 23% the week after Thanksgiving. Severe weather problems also contributed to the dilemma of unexpected package volumes. Delivery volume per day during that period rose 14% or about twice UPS's expectations. More than 70 retailers promoted next-day delivery on orders placed as late as 11:00 pm on December 23, overwhelming UPS systems and sorting facilities.

The impact of these unexpected lapses in meeting customer expectations were significant for UPS. Customer relationship issues aside, its 4th Quarter 2013 financial results included:

- $150 Million in costs related to the delivery problems
- $50 Million in refunds to customers
- Adjusted earnings decline of 8.5% compared with the previous year

The UPS response to these 2013 Christmas season delivery problems provide a classic example of using a *Strategic Initiative* approach to address a complex, challenging, and important business problem. It was not just a performance problem. It was a problem of multiple dimensions:

- Capacity
- Technology
- Staffing and training
- Facilities
- Customer partnering and volume forecasting
- Crisis management

UPS excels at executing strategic actions and initiatives. Its start-up (from zero to full operational certification) of the UPS Airline based in Louisville, KY to take on FedEx in the overnight shipment business in record time is a classic example.

In the case of the 2013 Christmas package delivery crisis, observe how UPS decided to approach its "Holiday Rush" initiative for 2014. A problem as complex as this would require a multi-dimensional, multi-technical, multi-operational, multi-functional, and highly-coordinated effort.

Sponsored at the highest levels of UPS, these integrated actions became the key elements (or Projects) deemed necessary to not only prevent a recurrence of the 2013 debacle, but to move UPS to new levels of performance capability.

- Bolstering shipment network capacity through facility expansions, process automation, job simplification, and faster implementation of technology
- Ramping up hub modernization efforts
- Developing more predictive volume planning models that incorporate changing consumer behavior and sales promotions
- Expediting the rollout of proprietary On Road, Integrated, Optimization, and Navigation software (ORION) with the goal of embedding the technology into 45% of U.S. driver routes by the end of 2014 – almost double the original plan
- Improving collaboration with large customers to create better visibility of every incoming package even before our customers' trucks arrive at our facilities

On December 25, 2014, *The Atlanta Journal,* where UPS is headquartered, reported that "UPS has spent $500 million to prepare for the holidays and expand capacity for the future, including new sorting facilities, temporary facilities and new technology such as a system to scan boxes on all six sides. According to ShipMatrix data, UPS Express had 99% on-time performance for Monday and Tuesday this week."[5]

The Wall Street Journal also reported on results of the UPS initiative at the end of 2014.

"UPS will deliver more than 34 million packages on December 22, more than any other in its history. To avoid a repeat of last year's embarrassing and costly debacle, it has spent about $500 million preparing for the holidays with projects including automated sorting systems to rapidly identify ZIP Codes and swiftly reroute packages in the event of bad weather. That automated system – known as its 'Next Generation Sort Aisle' – is now operating in three hubs around the country. The new technology scans packages and quickly flashes instructions to workers so they can process 15% more packages a day (or as many as 47,000 an hour). UPS hopes to lower its cost per package and improve the productivity of its more than 400,000 global employees, while reducing the over $500 million it spends a year training those workers by simplifying their tasks. Another of UPS's biggest initiatives is a continuing modernization of its oldest hubs. The Next Generation Sorting Aisle is now central to that goal."[6]

As we will outline in chapter nine, a significant strategic initiative typically requires multiple projects, project teams, and strong, coordinated project leadership. Due to the focus, cross-functional collaboration, sponsorship, willingness to invest, program or project management, and accountability involved in the UPS example, it is noteworthy in comparing it to our concept and model for using a strategic initiative portfolio and project management as a logical and effective methodology for reliably accomplishing strategic goals.

The Affordable Health Care Act's Website Deployment as a Strategic Initiative

After the Obama administration began in 2008, it could be argued that no single domestic strategic initiative was more important to the administration and the American people than passage of the 2010 Affordable

Care Act (ACA) – and its highly visible implementation via HealthCare.gov. And while the merits of the law itself and its features may be debated for years to come, the jury is already in on how this critically important and costly initiative was led and implemented.

The Wall Street Journal reported some rather disturbing facts and conclusions after reviewing a report issued by the Inspector General's Office of the Department of Health & Human Services (HHS).[7] Most of these facts are related to development and deployment of the critically important HealthCare.gov web site which is the primary web-based platform for people who need to buy insurance and apply for tax credits under the ACA.

1. The federal government skipped key contracting requirements when awarding hundreds of millions of dollars to build the HealthCare.gov site.

2. The government failed to fully probe the past performance of the key contractor (GCI Federal, a Canadian IT firm) and other contractors.

3. The site was built with thirty-three companies holding sixty contracts, but the Centers for Medicare and Medicaid Services (CMS) did not designate one single company to coordinate contractor activities.

4. Several big contracts, including the one with the Canadian firm, ballooned to two or three times the initially estimated costs. The Canadian contract swelled from $58 million to $207 million.

5. Federal officials drafted and accepted agreements that left the government on the hook for whatever it cost for the contractors to complete their work.

6. The CMS unit tasked with building the site paints a picture of rushed and sloppy work with poor oversight that did not meet the agencies' standards.

7. The HealthCare.gov site launched in 2013 with many problems that initially crippled enrollments by consumers.

8. As of February 2014, the government had committed to paying $800 million for contracts for the site and the total cost as of January 2015 is still unknown.

The government has made many changes to rectify some of the above issues, including appointment of consulting firm Accenture to manage and coordinate the overall HealthCare.gov deployment.

It would be easy to write off many of the problems revealed by the Inspector General's report as typical government inefficiency. However, the truth is that this was a classic example of an organization's inability to execute on a vital strategic initiative. In the (lack of) process, it did incalculable damage to the organization and its leaders, not to mention the impact on the perceptions of the organization in the eyes of its citizen consumers.

Many lessons can be learned here, and while some of CMS's failures to execute seem extreme in magnitude, they are by no means unusual in terms of their root causes.

- Inadequately detailed planning and goal setting
- Failure to properly define performance and capability requirements in advance
- Absence of experience in delivering on similar initiatives of similar magnitude
- Inadequate oversight of contractors
- Use of unqualified contractors or internal staff
- Lack of program management
- Lack of proper testing and piloting of key technology elements

- Lack of key sponsor involvement and knowledge
- Failure to define key outcomes
- Failure to define and achieve critical milestones of progress
- Lack of accountability for success
- Failure to recognize and admit problems and shortcomings of the initiative in time to rectify them
- Cost overruns and lack cost controls
- Lack of an effective and involved steering committee

With complex strategic initiatives such as the two we have described, just a few of these critical issues not being proactively addressed can spell the difference between success and failure.

Obviously, strategic initiatives can be quite complex and require considerable planning and ongoing management. Let's address the activities required for key initiative formation.

Key Steps for Forming Strategic Initiatives

During the previous planning stage, strategic imperatives and goals were defined and agreed on by the executive team. These strategies and goals came about as the executives pondered the implications of data shared from their common fact base and determined what to do about critical issues and important opportunities facing the organization.

Strategic Initiatives are logical, action-oriented extensions of Strategic Goals and Imperatives. They are the mechanism and focused efforts by which an organization translates strategic goals and imperatives to action.

Multiple strategic initiatives will often be underway at once, some from the current year and others potentially continuing from previous planning cycles. The collection of these in-process initiatives represents the organization's Strategic Initiatives Portfolio.

The initiatives portfolio should be reviewed periodically (always in light of current business conditions and events) to ensure ongoing commitment to and support for the initiatives. Anything that is considered to be of strategic value and importance to the business can be the focus of a strategic initiative. Those that arise from the strategic goals and imperatives discussed previously are most likely to be formalized.

Often, strategic initiatives are related to future product, future service, future technology, or future direction. That does not mean that today's existing business processes or challenges should not be the focus of a strategic initiative. We believe there is great value in balancing the initiatives portfolio between both current and future opportunities.

Boeing Company, for example, is re-thinking its formula for innovation. In the past, developing new technologies was reserved for big projects every fifteen years or so to build the fastest and farthest-flying jetliners like the 787 Dreamliner.

Today, Boeing centers innovation on incremental improvements that will make it possible to deliver aircraft more quickly to airlines – with greater reliability and at a lower price. Boeing is innovating to make aircraft design more simplistic and its jets more reliable. Boeing's initiative extends to every corner of its operations. It is aggressively trying to renegotiate contracts with suppliers in a push toward faster, better, and cheaper production. CEO, Ray Conner, says Boeing's priority now is completing its current slate of seven projects on time and on budget.

Regardless of the focus for each individual initiative to be included in the portfolio, the process for forming, defining, and documenting them is similar. Taking each strategic imperative in turn, the team now names and defines each strategic initiative to be added to the Portfolio of Initiatives to be adopted and carried out. The sequence for progressing from common data sharing to strategic initiative formation might look something like the following progression of logical and strategic thinking:

Strategic Initiative A: Core Customer Online Offering Development (example)

	Initiative A	Facts & Assumptions
1	**Common Fact Base Issue**	Uncertainty – lack of plan for primary sources of future growth; lack of new and more attractive products for core customers
2	**Primary Implication(s)**	Unable to decide on longer range plans for growth areas and product development; unacceptable gap between current trajectory and needed goals
3	**Strategic Imperative**	New products are required to drive better returns from current core customers (given "new era" balance sheet constraints); focus must be on secure online products
4	**Strategic Goal**	Devote scarce balance sheet resources to servicing (and earning better returns from) our best, core customers
5	**Strategic Initiative**	Develop more profitable new product offering(s) for core customers; *"Core Customer Online Offering Initiative"*
6	**Key Metric(s)**	-New product with 10% better margins than existing offerings for core customers -Balance sheet ratio improvement -Time to market
7	**Major Milestone(s)**	Team defined within 10 days; viable new product options analysis (revenue, cost) done and ready to present within 90 days; decision within 120 days

Carefully recording or documenting the thought process of initiative formation in this summarized manner provides concise information about progression from common fact base identification to strategic initiative formation. This documentation is useful because it:

- Captures primary assumptions that underlie the decision to form the strategic initiative
- Summarizes in sequence the logic used to define the initiative
- Defines preliminary metrics to be used for initiative formation and tracking

162

- Provides key facts and information with which to communicate about the initiative internally
- Becomes a tool for ongoing management and monitoring of the initiative as it forms and progresses

A Comment about the Assumptions that Underlie Strategies

We have acknowledged that future-oriented decisions and plans always rely on assumptions. The question is: "How good or accurate are our assumptions?" We have also discussed the importance of a common fact base grounded in "evidence" and advocated documenting the key assumptions being used as factors in (or basis for) strategic decisions – in order to create a decision-making audit trail. Why? So that as time passes we are able to reconstruct how and why we arrived at strategic decisions. Further, we know that the outcomes of major decisions are often more sensitive to some assumptions than others. (For example, assumptions about competitor pricing strategies may be more important to strategic success than our assumptions about overall economic growth.) Therefore, as part of the process for documenting assumptions we should include the beliefs we hold about which of our assumptions will be most critical to monitor over time.

One thing we can say with virtual certainty is that some of our assumptions will be wrong, as a perfect view of the future is not possible. Any assumption having a large effect on outcomes should be examined via uncertainty analysis – basically, examining both more pessimistic and optimistic possibilities than those used as the base assumption. The key is to identify when our plans are most likely to break down, particularly in pessimistic scenarios. We want to know when the profitability of a venture will become negative and at what point we should abandon or postpone the venture – even if significant resources have already been allocated or consumed. This will help identify key decision points or "go or no-go" milestones. Acknowledging an acceptable range of uncertainty for key assumptions before undertaking the initiative and then making it clear to all stakeholders is good practice. By deciding ahead of time to abandon, postpone, or reformulate the initiative if out-of-range conditions occur, we can better combat a common strategic error – the error of allowing inertia rather than current facts to drive major initiatives forward.

Prioritizing Strategic Initiatives

There are almost always more proposed candidates for strategic initiative formation than the organization's resources, whether financial or human, can realistically support. Following an objective process for initiative selection and prioritization is preferable to biting off too much at a time, thereby preventing overreach and over-commitment.

Prioritization can be tricky, since individual executives, functions, and business units often have their own preferred actions and strategies, which they genuinely believe will best benefit the organization. Remembering how important it is for the executives to be aligned around the overall strategy and the initiatives that will translate it to action, consensus on the *process* for key initiative prioritization and selection is most critical.

Earlier we discussed a set of characteristics or qualifications for actions rising to the status of a strategic initiative. We must again recognize that there may be any number of potential strategic actions that could rise to this level, again necessitating the need for an objective prioritization process.

Many techniques can be used to select between a set of good alternatives. Simple voting is one approach. Rating and ranking can also be used. Experience has shown that making the alternatives *objectively visible* is a good way to present and discuss available alternatives. Combining the discussions of strategic actions and criteria into a single dialogue is often more successful than simply debating based on biases and personal preferences.

Strategic Initiative Prioritization Matrix

Let's look at an example of a matrix that is helpful for facilitating initiative prioritization discussions. The matrix makes the options more visible and juxtaposes them with their assumed outcomes. A sample matrix is shown below. If executives can agree on where each candidate initiative belongs on the matrix, you are more likely to reach agreement on which initiatives you want to adopt, fund, and execute.

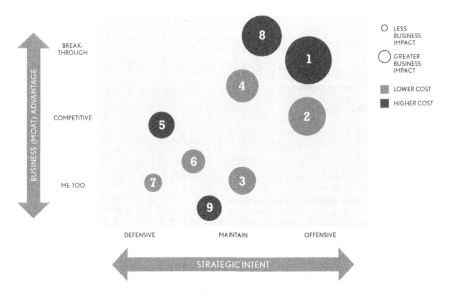

Strategic Initiatives Prioritization Matrix

In this case, we are attempting to choose three or four final initiatives from nine candidates.

Decision criteria in this example include:

- The anticipated impact on our competitive advantage as a business (breakthrough vs. merely competitive).
- The projected magnitude of the benefits to the business.
- The degree to which we are being reactive or proactive in our strategic initiatives or actions (defensive vs. offensive).
- The assumed cost of deploying the initiative – relative to other initiative choices.

Often the selected initiatives are a combination of offensive and defensive, rather than just one or the other. Typically, you need to take defensive action immediately (such as data or network security) while working through more ground-breaking solutions (like a new, more technically innovative product line).

For example, in the investment advisory business, three new software-based, automated investment advisors have recently emerged: Future Advisor, Rebalance IRA, and Wealthfront. They provide low-cost, quality alternatives to traditional investment advisors. The services offered by the new computer-based advisors are not second rate. Client accounts can receive daily monitoring and management rather than the quarterly or annual reviews provided by many traditional advisers. Every trade is automatically vetted against the investment strategy promised to the client. And investors pay less, not more for the services they receive – usually only 0.25%, rather than the 1% traditional advisors charge.[8] Not surprisingly, firms like Charles Schwab and Vanguard are now investing heavily in technology to provide high-quality, fiduciary service to small investors. These are defensive moves.

Initiatives that help create or increase business *moat* advantage are more likely to be those that incorporate technology advances or patentable ideas and methods that are difficult for competitors to match or overcome. Investment firms are typically *narrow moat* businesses.

The x and y axes on our initiative prioritization matrix will vary somewhat according to the nature of the business and its circumstances. Anticipated *Business Benefit* or *ROI* and *Level of Effort* are often used as the two axes, with the size of the bubbles representing relative magnitude of benefit.

The important point here is that, insofar as possible, the entire strategic planning and executive team should be involved in choosing the strategic initiatives. The better aligned and committed they are to these actionable thrusts of the strategic plan, the more likely the plan is to succeed.

Again we can turn to UPS as an example of selecting a business-critical strategic initiative, followed by focused, collaborative, cross-functional program management and execution. We described previously in this chapter the challenges faced by UPS at the end of 2013, when they were beset with holiday package processing capacity and late delivery problems, resulting in hits to their reputation as well as to their financial results.

A February 2016 *Atlanta Journal* article headline reads, "UPS enjoys holiday surge; Shipping giant's 4th quarter 2015 profit tripled as it avoided year-end snags." The company's home town newspaper further reported, "After largely avoiding the holiday snags of the previous two years, UPS said its fourth quarter profit tripled to $1.3 billion. The year-end profit surge helped the company post an annual profit of $4.8 billion, up from $3 billion in 2014. During the holiday peak season, UPS delivered 612 million packages, up 7% and a record for the company."[9] In this case a strategic initiative was badly needed – and it "delivered."

Can "People" Be Strategic Initiatives?

Years ago, the legendary management consultant Peter Drucker said, "The yield from the human resource really determines the organization's performance." Before finalizing a portfolio of strategic initiatives, the executive team may want to pause long enough to ask this simple question:

Can our most important strategic goals and initiatives be accomplished without greater focus and emphasis on engaging, informing, developing, and motivating our people?

If the answer to that question is no, then a people-focused strategic initiative may be called for. Such an initiative, if chosen, should leverage – but not be led by – the HR function, for a variety of reasons. A people-focused strategic initiative should have a non-HR executive sponsor if the organization is to take it seriously. Otherwise it risks being viewed simply as business as usual.

A recent Wall Street Journal article sub-heading read, "The best managed companies excel in employee engagement and development." Making the argument that people are a key factor in driving a company's results, it cites a Drucker Institute multi-year study of 693 companies which compares their performance improvement (or decline) across five major factors:

- Employee Engagement & Development
- Financial Strength
- Customer Satisfaction
- Innovation
- Social Responsibility

each of the five factors contain multiple components, all of which we won't attempt to discuss here. But as it turns out, the fifty companies that had the best improvement in their employee engagement score also produced more positive results in the other four factors. The key elements affecting employee engagement success include:

- How well a company conveys to its workers a vision and sense of mission

- Its pay and benefits levels
- Job satisfaction
- Opportunities for training and promotion

The people resourcing of strategic initiatives must be thought of as a key success factor in the execution of a business strategy. A pause to consider elements of the above-mentioned study may be helpful in judging, from the beginning, the likely success of the company's initiative execution effort.

Chapter 8 - Strategic Initiatives Formation
Key Thoughts & Takeaways

Before proceeding to the next chapter, please take a few minutes to think about the following with your organization in mind:

What are my key takeaways from this chapter?

What issues have I observed in my company or organization?

What are the implications for my organization?

9. Strategic Initiative Execution

A Few Words on Execution

"It's impossible to have a good strategy poorly executed. That's because execution actually *is* strategy – trying to separate the two only leads to confusion."

That's the opening sentence from an article entitled "Stop Distinguishing between Strategy and Execution," by Roger L. Martin at the University of Toronto.

He goes on to say "Blaming poor execution for the failure of your 'brilliant' strategy is a part of what I've termed 'The Execution Trap' – how 'brilliant' can your strategy really be if it wasn't implementable?" This article led to a lot of discussion between the authors, leading to productively examining a host of problems we've seen over the years.

If we were to re-state what he's getting at, it might be something like this.

A strategy isn't a strategy without:

- The organization clearly understanding what it is (including the *why*)
- Boundary conditions explaining the way to play
- Tangible objectives which establish expectations

In other words, a strategy as well as an agreed on forward path must be articulated in a way that enables opportunity generation, decision making, and management throughout the organization.

David J. Collins and Michael G. Rukstad, in an *HBR* article entitled, "Can You State What Your Strategy Is?" say, "...companies that don't have a simple and clear statement of strategy are likely to fall into the sorry category of those that have failed to execute their strategy, or worse, those that never even had one."

Collins and Rukstad speak of an "actionable strategic statement" that is specific, measurable, and time bound. They further claim that it should be a single goal that drives the operation of the business over the next several years. It should define a scope to "make it obvious to managers which activities they should concentrate on and, more important, which they should not do."

Earlier, we outlined a process for establishing a *common fact base* to provide context for the organization in terms of its business environment, competition, and possible futures. The set of facts in turn suggest potential implications, which collectively lead to insight and then ultimately to strategic imperatives, decisions, and actions. Collins and Rukstad's article supports this thesis, as well as many other elements of the pragmatic planning model we are advocating. They state:

> *...a great strategy...requires careful evaluation of the industry landscape...It also calls for an analysis of competitors' current strategies and a prediction of how they might change in the future. The process must involve a rigorous, objective assessment of the firm's capabilities and resources and those of competitors...We have found that one of the best ways to do this is to develop two or three plausible but very different strategic options... The wording of the strategy statement should be worked through in painstaking detail. In fact, that can be the most powerful part of the strategy development process.... It should be accompanied by detailed annotations that elucidate the strategy's nuances (to preempt any possible misreading) and spell out its implications.*

While Collins' and Rukstad's comments are more narrowly aimed at reaching a succinct strategy statement, the objective we seek is instead – *an actionable strategic plan*. Part of the "detailed annotations" required for a complete plan are a defined portfolio of strategic initiatives which then make self-evident the most critical actions on which the company will be focusing.

No strategy or initiatives are sacrosanct. While the timeframe of a strategic plan is naturally multi-year, the strategy should be examined via the process we have suggested each year – and the portfolio of strategic initiatives defined should also be reviewed to ensure any one of them is not diverting attention away from something else that may have become more pressing.

We say this to illustrate a point. Execution of strategic initiatives should not be the "choiceless doing" which Roger L. Martin claims is the natural result of trying to define strategy as "deciding what to do," and execution as "doing the thing the strategists decided."

More on Execution

One of the authors has been heard to say during his many "soapbox" moments, "Good assets can be ruined by poor execution, but poor assets cannot be salvaged by superior execution." A project or investment opportunity can be executed in stellar fashion, with timelines met and costs under control, but if the premise of the project was based on bad information or flawed logic, superior execution becomes merely a way to minimize loss. Thought of in this way, execution is a *maximizing* exercise, in that it maximizes the profits of good investments and minimizes the losses in poor investments. Either way you look at it, execution is crucial.

The foregoing thoughts can be virtually duplicated verbatim, but by changing the word "asset" or "project" with the word strategy. Rarely will anyone undertake a project if there is no demonstrated value proposition and without a reasonably clear understanding of how it will be accomplished. Likewise, a strategy without an executable forward plan isn't workable. Said differently, strategy must include *tangible objectives* and an *understandable, agreed on forward path*.

Let's contemplate a hypothetical company with a representation of its strategy on a single slide. This slide is used internally by management to communicate to employees as well as to Wall Street the direction of the company. One element of the strategy is "grow organically." The CEO talks about it on multiple occasions and believes it is crystal clear. On the surface it is a clear statement of a choice or intent. However, there is no information in the presentation providing any *tangible* plans for where the growth is going to come from. Any assets under development will be completed within the next year or so, and no clear commitment is made to ensure additional opportunities will materialize or become profitably available. In such a situation, employees and investors are essentially asked to *trust* that the CEO will make it happen.

It may well be the case that all will eventually be as envisioned in the CEO's mind; however, Wall Street will not assign value to unproven track records and non-existent opportunities. Likewise, employees will not feel confident if they don't understand where they're headed, especially if it is obvious what competitors are doing. Even if the CEO is given the benefit of doubt for a period of time, patience will eventually disappear if a forward plan is not presented. The strategy in such a situation is not complete. In fact, it is simply a statement of position: *This is who we are.*

But strategy and valuation are both about the future. For both internal and external worlds to understand the company and its potential, the strategy must also illustrate:

- This is our view of the future.
- This is our plan or forecast.
- This is who we will become (and how we will evolve).

If this cannot be explained in tangible terms supported by numbers, opportunities, and capabilities, then the strategy – by definition, related to the future – is not a viable strategy.

In this sense, we agree with Roger L. Martin's contention that there should be no distinction between strategy and execution. A strategy without a requisite implementation path "built in" will never be clear, and a strategy which cannot handle less than perfect execution will not deliver on value.

If you still insist that strategy and execution be thought of as separate, consider the following analogy. The coach of a football or soccer team clearly has a vision for how his team will be most successful. He is familiar with the resources at his disposal, chooses which players will start or lead. He designs *plays* or *tactics* to use during a game and drills his players so they understand their individual roles in each play. He customizes his *set of plays* or approach depending on the next opponent he will face. He puts a plan in place and lets everyone on the team know how they will approach the opponent and how he or she intends to win.

But despite all preparations, in the real world of competition, the contest almost never proceeds exactly as planned. Thus, the team must be able to adapt to the competition during the course of the game and only periodically regroup with the coach. There is no "choiceless doing" during a game. Thus, the *boundaries* of "choiceful doing" must be clear. The players must understand to what extent they are allowed to improvise – and that they are *expected* to make adjustments. Each team will be different depending on the personalities, experience, and abilities of the coach and his or her players, as well as other resources available. Some game plans may assume or allow for a large degree of improvisation, while others may be more rigid. In all cases, the players will be forced to adapt to what is happening on the field.

Boundary Conditions

We mention above the concept of "boundary conditions that explain the way to play." When employees clearly understand what must be accomplished – the strategic imperatives and initiatives – their potential can be unleashed. Appropriate boundary conditions empower them to make decisions and follow opportunities consistent with the company's way to play.

For example, if a department is simply asked to "deliver more opportunities" in their area without defined criteria for those opportunities, the results may prove unprofitable. Likewise, employees may become discouraged if the opportunities, believed to be consistent with the request, are later turned down for not meeting *unspoken* expectations. On the other hand, if investment criteria are clear, such that the department can itself screen opportunities appropriately, then those which pass the test will more likely be profitable. Valuable organizational effort and management attention will not be wasted.

ExxonMobil is a great example in this regard. The company has traditionally maintained very high investment standards when compared with other companies in its industry. The exact expectations (or target metrics) change each year, but these expectations are clearly communicated to those considered *opportunity generators.* Engineers, geologists, chemists, and marketers are constantly managing their base business to meet expense targets and are continually seeking new development opportunities. They know what they're looking for, and the level of financial literacy is high, because the metrics expected are clearly communicated and are a topic of ongoing conversations.

Economics (or discounted cash flow and ratio analysis) are performed on every discretionary capital or maintenance project. The more significant projects must stand up to peer review. And because standards are high, many opportunities which other companies would likely pursue are screened out as not meeting the requisite standard. This is done by the very people who are coming up with the ideas or by peer review. Because of this standard, management can stay focused on the most important issues.

But most important of all, ExxonMobil rarely undertakes unprofitable projects. As we discussed earlier, their good projects are no better than anyone else's good projects, but they have far fewer failed projects than most other companies. Because of this, ExxonMobil's return on capital employed is rarely matched by other companies in the industry and is unmatched when considered over many decades.

The Strategic Initiative Portfolio

Part of the reason to define strategic objectives is to illuminate the firm's primary areas of focus. Any major activity important to the firm's medium-term future can potentially fit under the umbrella of strategic initiatives. In the previous chapter, we provided a set of criteria and key steps required to form strategic initiatives. If followed, each initiative will be justified, put in context, including clear objectives and metrics. So where do the initiatives come from, or what should be their focus?

Certain categories of initiatives are highly likely to at least be a part of the portfolio in some form or fashion, though details from year to year will vary. A few examples worth mentioning are:

- **Existing Business Optimization** – operational efficiency, re-focusing efforts, cost elimination, service level, process improvement, etc.

- **Growth & Investment** – Investment level and return required, new market entry, strategic contract negotiation with key business partner, contingency plan, monitoring current year results versus expectations in order to make adjustments in the future, etc.

- **Organizational Change or Improvement** – Ensuring alignment between strategic imperatives or goals and organizational incentives or capabilities, employee satisfaction, recruiting and retention, succession, etc.

Paramount to managing a *portfolio* of strategic initiatives is making sure that the initiatives pursued are, in fact, *the* most important things on which the company should focus. In the previous chapter, we introduced the concept of initiative prioritization. It might seem as if this is a one-time or up-front activity. We want to emphasize that the same process should be conducted each year, and in any given year, the results may indicate that one of the initiatives selected in a previous cycle may have become a lower priority since it was defined and chosen. Managing the strategic initiatives portfolio means that the firm is objectively willing to disinvest in a particular initiative or area in favor of that which is most important now.

It can be extremely difficult to slow down or halt progress on something that seemed so important previously and which likely remains quite important. Consider the characteristics of strategic initiatives described earlier: they are high priority, sponsored by a top executive, led by a senior executive, and attract some of the organization's best people. Wouldn't we want our best people on the toughest and most important projects? When an initiative becomes less of a priority, a choice can be made to delegate to leadership lower in the organization, significantly lengthen the timeline, outsource, place on standby, or stop altogether. Whatever the choice, management must be willing to make the hard decision to deprioritize what was previously considered a top priority.

Strategic Initiatives Portfolio Prioritization & Visibility Enable Achievement

Previously, we discussed the need for a process to select strategic initiatives the business will commit itself to in pursuit of its strategic imperatives and goals. In addition to the need to initially select the initiatives, you also need to prioritize and track the initiatives for deployment and project management purposes. It is important for the organization and its people to have ongoing visibility to the initiatives, as well as to how the initiatives relate to each other. In practice, a snapshot of a portfolio of strategic initiatives A, B, C, D, and E might look something like this:

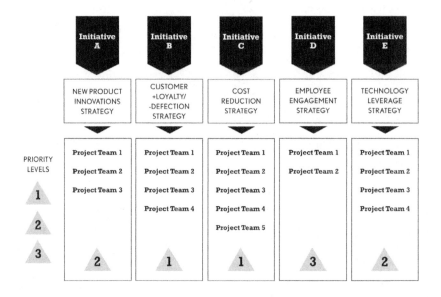

A set of five initiatives such as those described in this example are almost never of equal importance – or urgency. What is required, however, is that the relative importance or urgency of the initiatives one to another is both clear and understood by everyone involved.

In this case, the executive team has determined that Initiative B (Customer Loyalty or Defection Strategy) and Initiative C (Cost Reduction Strategy) are its highest priorities. This does not mean that Initiatives A, D, and E are not important. On the contrary, these initiatives are also strategically important and should be funded, resourced, and undertaken. But for various reasons (financial, timing, resource constraints, or otherwise) initiatives B and C receive preferential attention. This focus is illustrated in the above example by the fact that the two highest priority initiatives have more project teams engaged. This fact is likely to remain so unless and until the organization's priorities are reconsidered. Until such time these five initiatives represent the vital few action-oriented strategies the business will pursue to deliver on its future. They are the mechanism by which the business achieves its most critical objectives.

Successfully managing five or more strategic initiatives in parallel will challenge most organizations. The chosen initiatives need to consider ongoing changes in circumstances, challenges, people, urgency, and so on. To keep the business's executives focused on the firm's strategic initiatives, the portfolio needs to be actively monitored and assessed. Capable people as well as good portfolio and project management tools and techniques will, without doubt, be required to accomplish this.

Portfolio and Project Management

In addition to ensuring the portfolio of initiatives represents the key priorities of the organization, it must be managed as any other valuable portfolio. This includes reporting on metrics which represent progress and overall results. Overall metrics can also be represented by a performance dashboard, which would be assembled, drawing appropriate metrics from each individual initiative in a format readily consumable by senior management.

Portfolio reporting might come from an enterprise-level project management office (E-PMO). This office would be responsible for both standardized and custom reporting requirements. As the initiatives will make heavy use of executive, management, and other human resources from across the organization, a key role of the E-PMO is to ensure timelines are feasible, while also pointing out potential conflicts which may, for example, be coming down the road from Initiative A due to the requirements of Initiative B or even routine but particularly intense base business needs.

Strategic initiatives, almost by definition, are multi-threaded projects, and as such, should follow good project management practices. Project managers for each initiative would work closely with the E-PMO to fulfill that office's standard reporting requirements, as well as to agree on any special reporting requirements for a given initiative. The project manager should track time and resources, timelines, and milestones; clearly identify key next steps and potential risks; highlight temporal proximity to major decision points; and finally, keep participants aligned by establishing and scheduling regular status meetings. (Remember the issues related to the Affordable Health Care Act website deployment?)

Execution: A Brief Review

A brief review of our execution discussion is in order before a more detailed discussion regarding metrics and critical success factors. Thus far, we have focused on the following:

- Importance of an understandable forward path in order for strategy decisions to be successful and executable
- Necessity and reality of being flexible along the way – within understood boundaries
- Ensuring the portfolio of strategic initiatives is focused – and at times re-focused – on the most important opportunities and challenges facing the company
- Project management at both the initiatives portfolio and individual initiative levels

Mind the Metrics

Without discussing specific initiatives, it can be difficult to discuss the actual metrics that will be most useful while attempting execution. We can, however, mention general categories that exemplify the types of metrics we believe are most valuable at different stages of initiative progress and maturity.

It is helpful to consider different metrics at a minimum of four basic stages of strategic initiative progression or maturity.

- Early Stage = Leading Indicators
- Mid Stage = In-Process Indicators
- Advanced Stage = Output Indicators
- Completed Stage = Lagging or End Result Indicators

Related to each strategic initiative we propose creating or tracking at various stages of their maturity as follows:

Initiative Leading Indicators → Initiative In-Process Indicators → Initiative Output Indicators → End Result & Lagging Indicators

- ***Initiative Early-Stage Leading Indicators***, which at the beginning of initiative formation provide preparatory, early-stage milestones demonstrating that the project is appropriately ramping up:
  - Initiative-related Definitions
    - Initiative requirements and success factors
    - Required skills and competencies and an assessment of in house availability
    - Stated goals and deadlines
  - Initiative Plans
    - Leadership and staffing plan
    - Program plan and roadmap
    - Process milestones and metrics
- ***Initiative In-Process Indicators*** largely illustrate progress being made toward initiative direction, delivery, and decisions – early to mid-stage initiative maturity:

- o Key Milestones
  - Current state descriptions or illustrations
  - Design, such as architecture or pilot plans
  - Development schedule
- o Project management metrics
  - Status, timeline, milestones achievement
  - Spend vs. budget
- o Decisions:
  - Documented course corrections
  - Development and implementation plans
- *Initiative Output Indicators* provide indications or measures of preliminary results useful to the working team, steering committee, and potentially executive oversight outside of the project team.
  - o Observations – documentation of early observations which may or may not have already led to decisions about broader initiative deployment
  - o Conclusions – For example, if solutions to a major issue are sought and it is determined that three approaches should be tested, the conclusions related to the first approach and eventually the other approaches could be considered in process, and the final recommended approach would be an output.
  - o Results – for example, (1) preliminary results of early or final pilot testing or (2) actual costs of solution versus early-on estimates

- o Recommendations – for example, (1) move forward with implementation following successful pilot or (2) postpone implementation until major issues are resolved
- *Initiative End Result (Lagging) Indicators*, consist largely of metrics related to the major business metrics or opportunities the initiative was designed to impact. These are the metrics that will be tracked over the years to determine whether the strategy – and this element of the strategy in particular – was a success. Such metrics could include:
  - o Financial performance
  - o Market share improvements
  - o Business model impact
  - o Brand image changes
  - o Disruptive impact on the market or competitors

It should be apparent from the description above that not all metrics are useful or even available at all times during the process. Nor are all metrics useful to the broader audience outside of the working team and steering committee. However, thinking through useful key milestones, indicators, and metrics *up front* enables the team to define decision criteria and have more realistic expectations regarding what they must accomplish at each step along the way.

We cannot emphasize enough the importance of following the recommended steps for initiative formation – and developing indicators and metrics up front to provide foundational context for initiative execution. The initiative formation steps should include the motivating "why we're doing it" statement while simultaneously articulating preliminary goals, metrics, and milestones. Articulating a robust set of initiative indicators up front helps move the project forward and ensures you are planning for success and delivering results. These are the critical pieces of information necessary for aligning the steering committee and the working teams tasked with initiative delivery.

Initiative Milestones & Metrics Dashboard Required

Monitoring the progress (and the many activities, costs, and outcomes) of a major strategic initiative is a complex and challenging task. Managing multiple initiatives simultaneously is an even greater and more complex task. Using consistent, standardized methods and tools for tracking the progress of strategic initiatives should be viewed as a consequential part of the strategic planning and execution process. We recommend you develop or acquire such methods and tools. A simple, visual dashboard for each in-progress initiative should be used to track and review initiative status and progress. Using the various initiative maturity stages described earlier, a dashboard might contain data related to categories of information. The example below includes a variety of potential progress monitoring factor and metrics options.

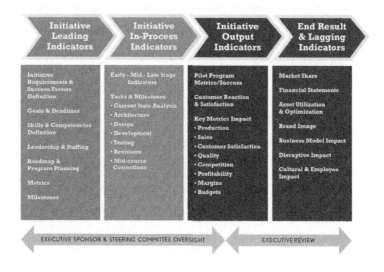

Such a dashboard must, of course, be customized for each organization and even for each individual initiative to be implemented. It needs to reflect the specifics of the initiative and the objectives it is planned to achieve. A key to the dashboard is to have assessed where the initiative needs to be (in terms of progress, metrics, and milestones) at each stage of its maturity. This assessment of progress vs. maturity is actually a milestone to be accomplished as one of the *leading indicators* of the initiative.

Having initiative dashboards allows for and helps facilitate regular oversight and review of initiative progress by executive management. Initially, at early formative stages of the initiative, oversight and review may be primarily accomplished at the steering committee or executive sponsor level. However, as the initiative progresses and matures, it will attract the attention of a broader slice of the organization's executives. After preliminary, pilot, or other early outcomes become apparent, decisions about accelerating, slowing down, or even halting initiatives need to be made. As these are the firm's most important and strategic initiatives, senior management needs and wants to be involved in decisions about the future of each one. The dashboard for each initiative becomes a helpful tool for managing the information required to support these decisions.

Executing on Strategic Initiatives: Critical Success Factors

Beyond the foundation provided via the formation process, critical execution success factors can be summarized by the acronym F.R.A.C.C., meaning: Focus, Resources, Advocacy, Communication, and Change Management. Let's review the nature and importance of each element:

- Focus: Assuring adequate attention to the strategic initiative

- o Members of the working team should each be able to dedicate as much as 50% of their time to the initiative.
- o Members of the steering committee should be able to dedicate as much as 25% of their time to the initiative, particularly in the early stages or until such time as it becomes clear their direct involvement can be reduced.
- o The leader of the working team should *not* function largely as the project tracker or person responsible for reporting, but should be focused on the core issues or opportunities central to the initiative. Administrative project tracking should be handled by another team member.
- Resources: Enabling the strategic initiative
  - o The steering committee for each committed initiative should include an executive sponsor and, at a minimum, the primary leader or subject matter expert(s) of the working team(s).
  - o In the case where an initiative requires undertaking something out of the ordinary, appropriate outside resources and expertise should be made available. The initiative leaders should be given time to develop a budget – almost starting with a blank check until proper scoping has been completed.
  - o Steering Committee members should make themselves available to the working team. Individual committee members should have an

open door policy. This is closely related to the next point.

- Advocacy: Championing the strategic initiative
  - The Committee must actively support the working team, acting as facilitators and advocates for them in relation to the rest of the organization.
    - The Steering Committee must help the working team manage upward at all times and must defend them vigorously, especially if expectations are inconsistent with real-life challenges – something that becomes clearer as the initiative progresses.
    - During or after implementation of any changes resulting from the initiative, the Executive Sponsor must make it clear to the rest of the organization that the working team has his or her full support and that any process changes are *the new way* to do business.
  - The Steering Committee should serve as ambassadors and champions of the initiative's objectives. This should be a natural role assuming the initiative formation approach suggested previously is followed, which includes context and the *why*.
  - Being a team member in a strategic initiative should culturally be perceived and publicly demonstrated to be a desirable role, leading to bigger and better things. A strategic initiative should not be the

> temporary home of *hot potato* employees for whom
> management is simply seeking a home

- Communication and Change Management: Preparing the organization for the strategic initiative

  o The committee needs to have real and substantive conversations with the working team rather than relying primarily on formal progress reports and red-yellow-green status updates. By "conversations," we mean true and healthy conversation back and forth, always with the aim of understanding and getting to the right answer.

  o The committee should make clear that adjustments to scope and approach are expected once more expertise is brought in and key issues crystallize.

  o Transitioning individuals, teams, and organizations to a desired future state – often known as "change management" – requires authoritative and frequent communication across the organization. Even the best-designed initiative will yield sub-optimal results if the intent, process, results, and potential impacts are not properly communicated and documented.

Focus & Resources

All parties must have the ability to focus appropriate attention on their respective initiatives. This is crucial. After all, strategic initiatives should be among the most important focus areas of the company. If competing priorities keep a member of the steering or working teams from focusing proper attention, clear but unspoken messages are sent. Either the initiative really isn't that important, or the initiatives carry downside risk to the participants. By downside risk, we refer to situations where stellar execution is necessary for merely satisfactory results, and if any bumps occur along the way, the participant will be negatively impacted or regarded. Such a no-win situation will dissuade high potential employees from wanting to participate in the future. Participants do not want to be in a situation where they are forced to perform one of their duties poorly and have it come back to haunt them later.

Steering Committee, Working Team, & Subject Matter Experts

As we have pointed out, the steering committee plays a pivotal role in initiative execution. The committee needs the right combination of organizational authority, expertise, and strong management, while simultaneously being flexible in approach and open to new ideas. In addition, working teams need to feel the steering committee is their advocate rather than taskmaster. When problems arise, as they inevitably will, working teams need to feel comfortable disclosing the full extent of the issues and in expressing candid opinions. Without this level of communication, safety, advocacy, and flexibility, the initiative's apparent or stated outcomes may not be all they seem to be or may come as a surprise to the wrong people at the wrong time.

The steering committee should include at least one member of the primary working team on the project. Our experience shows that the articulation of an initiative's purpose (or charter) is often seen to be in conflict with itself or may even be unworkable when developed without the help of those executing the initiative on a daily basis. At the very least, if the charter is developed lacking their input, the working team's first priority should be to review the charter and raise any concerns before proceeding.

Throughout the life of the project, the charter should be reviewed periodically to ensure that any new concerns are addressed as early as possible. One way is to make it a practice to review the charter prior to each significant review with the steering committee. It can be easy for the working teams to unintentionally migrate beyond the intended scope of the initiative and to forget a detail of the charter which may now seem inapplicable.

Communication & Change Management

When a major initiative is underway, people not directly involved with its efforts are often largely in the dark about what is going on and especially about how they may be impacted. *Outsiders* can have difficulty understanding that a lot of work has to be done before they see even a hint of the desired results. This is particularly true in cases where new software systems are involved at the enterprise scale with a custom implementation. The only thing outsiders may see are consultants crawling around, working teams demanding their time, and the impact to the monthly financials. All this business without immediately visible results can create a lot of impatience among those waiting to see delivery – including questions and concerns about "when it's going to be done" and "when will we have results." In addition, it is often difficult to imagine the post-project impacts on the way business will need to be done.

To keep everyone in the organization rowing in the same direction, proactive communication and well-designed change management plans must be integral parts of the up-front design. The simple fact is that people outside the initiative will seldom appreciate its impact and consequences until they are face to face with them – that is, unless it has been made abundantly clear at the time of approval, repeatedly while the project is underway, and again at the end. They assume the organization will keep doing exactly what they've been doing – same roles and positions. And at the end of the project, this "magic box" will produce amazing things with little to no effort.

Particularly toward the end of the project, many people around the organization need to be given detailed explanations and presentations about all the things that will change and how their jobs will be affected. Without this, people will resist, lack appreciation, misunderstand, and express irritation. These attitudes and misunderstandings can exist even with the best communication plan, but at least you can reduce the magnitude of impact.

We cannot overemphasize the importance of robust communication and change management planning in advance of strategic initiative deployment. People across the organization need to be informed and forewarned about:

- Project objectives and intended benefits to the company, timelines and milestones, major decision points, and the effort and costs involved

- Impact to them personally: What resources of theirs may be seconded to the project?

- Likely changes to the business processes they are familiar and comfortable with

- Post implementation resources required to sustain the project's intended results

- Periodic reminders of all the above, as well as reminders about progress to date and intermediate results (Remember that those outside the project aren't thinking too much about it, and new people in the organization may not have heard much of anything previously.)

If you are responsible for an initiative or the change management of an initiative, we cannot possibly list everything that needs to be considered, managed, and communicated for successful initiative adoption. Instead, we offer a short exercise to help you think through the issues:

Imagine yourself to be a manager who will be impacted by someone else's project – one that you are not part of. What if many things you are comfortable with and have been doing for years will now need to be done differently, but you are unsure about what "differently" means? Would you be surprised if you were told a new resource would be required in your department to comply with post-project requirements, especially if you are already being pressured on headcount? Do you even know why the project is being done? *What is it you need to know to give your full and committed support to a successful outcome?*

Case in Point: Enterprise Technology Initiative through the Lens of Critical Success Factors

An organization we worked with decided to embark on a major, enterprise-level business intelligence initiative. It would impact many facets of their financial planning and analysis (FP&A) processes, including monthly close, financial reporting, forecast updates, quarterly outlook, annual budget, and long-rang strategic planning. The reasons for undertaking this initiative were simple and straightforward, even though the project itself was very complex – something not fully appreciated at the time the executives decided to move forward. As might be expected, the company formed a steering committee and tasked it with bidding out the work to contractors. After the project was underway, we became involved primarily with a major sub-initiative concerning the strategic planning function – although due to the interconnected nature of the project, we also dealt with many issues associated with the larger initiative. Based on discussions with team members, as well as personal involvement, our observations highlight both the presence and absence of the FRACC critical success factors.

Focus: Working Team Conflicts

The internal subject matter expert (SME) responsible for the strategic planning sub-initiative was constantly being pressured to spend less time on the project. "Let the consultants do their job," he was told. From his perspective, he was letting the consultants focus on the very project elements for which they were experts, while he focused on the issues he alone understood as the internal SME. He could *not* spend less time on the project and still achieve the required results. His responsibilities were split to the point that he worked full time to deliver on his "day job" while leading a sizeable team of consultants and internal resources on the initiative. He already had a full time job, the responsibilities of which were not reduced while simultaneously leading the consultants and being required to deliver on the initiative. Thus, he lived in the office, often working until 2-3 am day after day including weekends.

Resources: Steering Committee Lacks Subject Matter Experts

We became involved at a time when the project had been properly envisioned and conceptually designed by the project leader mentioned above. We later found out, however, that this was actually the second time this same technology initiative was being tackled. The second effort was due to a significant scope deficiency issue the first time around. Originally, the steering committee was tasked largely with picking the vendor and forming the internal team. They also received infrequent updates and focused largely on progress versus timeline and budget. The SME's predecessor, when informed of the requirements of the strategic planning system, explained that the new long-range planning system as specified by the steering committee would in actuality *not* be useful to him for planning purposes. The former SME expressed concerns, but in the end was told he was to implement as requested. He was also told that the consultants would be able to execute the task as specified, and he would not need to be heavily involved in the project. Having clearly expressed his opinion, he felt obligated to execute "what the people paying him asked for" and moved forward.

Further complicating matters, the former SME was transferred to run a foreign office. The new SME was brought in as the new leader of the department and also tasked with implementing the new long-range planning system. He was similarly told that the project would not take up too much of his time and that he would mostly just need to be available to answer questions and provide periodic guidance. This did not turn out to be the case.

The very first time the SME was asked a question, the answer depended upon what the system was intended to deliver. Was the system supposed to do only A, or only B, or was it supposed to do both A and B? No one seemed to know the answer. He asked what was stated in the scope of the project that the now-working consultants had bid on. When the scope was reviewed, it was discovered that both A and B were to be accomplished by the system. The system they had been asked to build, could not deliver both A and B, so the scope conflicted with itself. To do both A and B required major changes to what the consultants had been asked to do.

It soon became apparent that the original task was understood neither by the steering committee, nor the consultants. The very people who would be primary users of the system had not been involved or been asked to provide appropriate input. The project had been ill-conceived, massively under-budgeted, and under-resourced, all because the people who most fully understood the task were not involved up front in the scoping and decision process. The SME had the unenviable task as new department leader of explaining to the steering committee and the consultants that their budget was only a quarter of what it should have been – and that massive changes were needed. The steering committee blamed the consultants for their cost estimate shortage. The consultants argued that these were scope changes.

They were, and they weren't. The simple fact was that the steering committee did not understand what they were asking for, and the consultants bid on what they understood they were being asked to do.

The project had progressed far enough that a real solution to these issues could not easily be implemented. Nevertheless everyone needed the project to move forward from where it was. In short, it had to be salvaged. Everyone did their best and produced something that delivered on *most* of what was needed. In the end, the solution was so complicated that, after producing the first annual plan via the system more than two years after the project was scoped, it was obvious that it was much too labor intensive to be a sustainable solution.

Advocacy: Getting the Right Support

After the SME salvaged and made good on the "mostly OK solution," he put together a presentation explaining to the CEO what the problems were and that the system he envisioned could be built to take advantage of other tools which already provided necessary base information, rather than recreating everything from scratch. He recommended a redesign that could deliver the project in half the time and at quarter of the cost of the original project, and the end solution would actually be useable. The CEO acknowledged that the SME was indeed the expert and approved the proposal. Two years' and millions of dollars' worth of round one work product were scrapped. The round two project that was scoped and approved, on the other hand, was completed on time and under budget.

Communication & Change Management: A Few Stumbles in Round Two

To keep everyone in the organization pulling in the same direction, proactive communication and well-designed change management plans must be integral parts of up-front initiative design. The struggles the SME had with management wanting him to spend less time on the project were partly his own doing. They resulted from him not making the requirements for his personal involvement absolutely clear when the project proposal was presented. The "why it is necessary" was clear, the design and consulting budget were clear, the timeline was clear, but what he did not explicitly cover was how much of his own time would be required during the project. He also did not make clear the resources that would be required to maintain the system going forward, other than in conversations that ensued during the presentation. Without rigorous questioning from management and without explicit explanation, these realities were simply not appreciated.

As the team neared the finish line for the project, during normal budgetary discussions, the SME presented general staffing requirements for the department. He mentioned that his department needed to have someone dedicated as the system expert, so that the department could use it as it was designed to be used. He was puzzled by the responses: "Can't we just have someone spend a quarter of their time administering the system?" In short, his answer was no. Then, "Well can it then be half time and make it a rotational responsibility within the department so one person doesn't have to specialize in it?" To the SME, a person heavily involved in the project, understanding its complexities and requirements, the answers were obvious. He couldn't understand why anyone would think they'd spent all this time, effort, and money building a system to deliver superior work products, yet assume there would be no need for anyone to be dedicated to its maintenance and use.

We repeat again a simple fact: *People outside the initiative will seldom appreciate its impact and consequences until they are face to face with them* – that is, unless it has been made clear at the time of approval, repeatedly while the project is underway, and again at the end.

Final Thoughts on Execution

Execution is tough work. Perhaps that's why it can be so tempting to separate execution from strategy, planning, and design. There is really only one dubious benefit from such separation: If we can compartmentalize these processes, then we can throw the ball over the fence and perhaps blame someone else for failure. As tempting as that is, we are compelled to acknowledge that a strategic plan is not workable without:

- Taking a position on the future
- A valid and quantifiable source of new or available opportunities
- Capabilities enabling us to take advantage of said opportunities
- An articulated, understandable, actionable path forward
- A workforce, board, and external shareholders who understand the big picture because the path forward is supported by data and has been explained in detail

Only when these pieces are in place can the company truly execute on the vision and direction of its leaders. Only when *all* the pieces are in place will the company deliver on its promises and realize the market value that management feels it deserves. Something we have been heard to say around earnings season and before "analyst day" is that the market wants to see three basic things:

- Management is competent – understands its business, knows what it is doing, and can speak the market's language
- Management is credible – says what it will do, then delivers what it says it will deliver
- Management has an executable path forward that can be valued numerically – with projections data illustrating future value creation

If the firm cannot make the financial markets comfortable by exhibiting these three things, then how can it ensure that its employees know what is expected? If employees are unclear on crucial deliverables, how can they achieve the desired results? A strategy that leaves out important details critical to its advancement will not result in the consistent long-term value creation envisioned by its developer(s), nor will it deliver a motivated workforce working toward the same objectives.

Following the pragmatic strategic planning process we have illustrated that focusing proper attention on the activities crucial to the company's success provides the framework necessary to develop, support, communicate, and deliver future value to shareholders and other stakeholders.

You may notice that we have spent more time talking about initiatives and execution than any other topic – *in a book focused on strategic planning.* Execution is that integral and that connected to strategy. A pragmatic approach to strategic planning requires that all the pieces come together as a well-defined, systematic, holistic process.

Chapter 9 – Strategic Initiative Execution
Key Thoughts & Takeaways

Before proceeding to the next chapter, please take a few minutes to think about the following with your organization in mind:

What are my key takeaways from this chapter?

What issues have I observed in my company or organization?

What are the implications for my organization?

10. Testing for Strategic Plan Viability

As stated in the preface, this book has been written to help organizations of almost any size create seven *essential conditions* under which strategic planning is more likely to be successful. In short, these seven conditions are:

- Practical, non-academic approach
- Clear, sequential process
- Right questions at the right time
- Objective decision-making criteria
- Aligned executives
- Reasonable portfolio of initiatives
- Self-honesty about realities

Throughout this book, we pose many questions primarily designed to give you something to think about, something to draw your mind to real issues your company may be facing. These are useful thought exercises. For this book to be useful to companies across industries and markets, it is difficult to present prescriptive details about how to put the *pragmatic* model into practice. In the end, many strategic planning process considerations can fit a particular company. Covering them all is beyond the scope of this book. The concepts in this book have addressed broad-range issues related to strategic planning and how to overcome them – ranging from how to gather and assess facts to organizational and alignment issues. We have even talked about the importance of examining the organization's fundamental business model. However, we have not yet provided detailed criteria or steps for assessing whether chosen strategic plans will accomplish all that you need them to. We now turn our attention to practical guidance about how to assess the *viability of the strategic plan itself.*

In discussing Common Fact Base & Analysis, we suggested as an early-stage planning activity the idea of assessing attitudes and knowledge about the organization's existing or past strategy. We said that one of the facts that needs to be held in common for a strategic planning team is a sense of *whether or not a current strategy and plan actually exists.* If one does exist, what perceptions exist about how successful it has been?

We hope we have made clear that for an executive team and all of their reports to move forward in a unified manner, they require a shared vision of the future. A shared vision is especially difficult to attain if the "path to achievement" of the vision has not been clearly or widely presented and analytically supported. At times, open debate is necessary to get all the issues out on the table. Without doing so, it is easy to *think* there is alignment: Executives we've worked with have understandably assumed that the path forward was crystal clear and that everyone was on the same page, but private discussions with key members of their staff and hallway conversations have often proven otherwise.

In addition to team alignment issues, we have discussed the importance of strategically focusing not only on the *existing business model* but also on the *future business model* needed for and applicable to future growth. These two business models are probably at least incrementally (if not dramatically) different. A singular focus on existing business and its related business model will open the company up to risk of disruption or technological stagnation. Likewise, a singular focus on the *new model* can lead a company to alienate existing customers or simply neglect what is often the largest current source of value and revenue.

Speaking of value, the entire purpose of *any* business is to create value for its customers and for its equity holders. Any strategic plan must demonstrate the expected value it is capable of creating over time. This is perhaps *the key* unifying element which has the ability to align not only executive management, but also employees, shareholders, board members, and the public investing community.

You need a way to help ensure you have a defined path forward, presented in such a way that everyone can get behind it – one which engenders confidence in all stakeholders. In short, you need:

- Assurance of understanding among management to enable execution
- An accurate idea of:
  - what our *base business* can be expected to deliver
  - what our *future growth plans* are expected to deliver
  - what together will deliver relative to required value creation objectives
- Assurance of plan feasibility
- Perspective about the need or significance of changes to our business model over time and the natural consequences of failure to evolve
- Aligned communication to all stakeholders

Below, we offer a practical way to *test* whether your strategic plans are perceived to be capable of satisfying these requirements. The test consists of five primary questions. Each is followed by the kind of supporting criteria or evidence that suggests whether you can satisfactorily proceed to the next question. In each case where evidence is lacking, we then suggest remedial action.

Testing for Strategy: Do We Really Have a Viable Strategy & Plan?

The characteristics of a viable strategic plan are straightforward. A viable plan will demonstrate in a convincing way that the firm will:

- Generate a sufficient profit
- At an appropriate or growing scale
- Repeatedly, and
- In the face of real constraints to the company, specifically:
    - Financial capacity
    - Market opportunity
    - Execution capacity

Strategy Viability Framework: Context for Viability Test

The graphic at the beginning of this chapter, which we call the Strategy Viability Framework, illustrates these characteristics. The inner triangle shows the primary balanced business model objectives as discussed in chapter 4 (Business Model Assessment). It reminds us that a company must:

- Operate within a sustainable (repeatable) model, maintaining a sufficient and visible *hopper* of opportunities in order to keep doing what it's now doing
- Grow by virtue of a combination of:
    - Its existing business or business model
    - Its emerging or new business model
- Do so in a way that ensures the profitability of all existing operations:

      o   Cutting unprofitable units which no longer contribute positively to the whole

      o   Investing in new opportunities which deliver returns well in excess of their cost of capital

The outer triangle shows that each of these activities is pursued in the face of multiple constraints. A company's repeatability is constrained by: (1) its financial capacity to access new opportunities that fit its business model and (2) which opportunities are available in sufficient quantities. Profitability depends on the firm having an accurate view of available market and investment opportunities and on its ability to secure and execute those opportunities. Growth depends on demonstrating that it can reliably execute (produce the results it envisions) available opportunities at a scale and pace within financial constraints.

Strategy Viability Test

As a way to assess the success of the strategic planning effort in your organization, we offer five straight-forward questions to consider – or perhaps pose to your organization's leaders.

Question 1 – What is our strategic plan?

Evidence of the existence of a well-understood strategic plan to include:

- Clearly explainable and succinct statements of strategy
- Broad understanding of strategy by both internal and external audiences
- Identified tangible strategic opportunities, goals, and actions
- Progress being made against the organization's primary goals and challenges
- Close alignment of the senior management team around strategic imperatives, goals, and initiatives

Remediation Actions

If the above conditions do not exist (lack evidence), then further strategy articulation is called for.

Question 2 – Are our strategic plans working?

Evidence of a viable strategic plan:

- Articulated view of the future exists, supported by appropriate analysis, including future scenarios that illustrate value creation in the context of:
  - Market conditions
  - Competitive landscape
  - Potential or existing disruptions
  - Other uncertainties
- Strategic plan includes tangible actions directly associated with key strategy elements.
- The impact of these tangible actions can be numerically forecasted via predictable revenue streams from known opportunities, assets, initiatives, and projects.
- Each major strategic action *individually* delivers positive shareholder value or can be shown to improve strategic position, mitigate a significant risk, or deliver other definable benefits at an understood reasonable cost.
- The sum total of base business *(such as current operations)* and all incremental actions *(planned actions and initiatives)* combine to deliver future shareholder value equal to or greater than that indicated by the minimally required share price trajectory (share price growth at the company's cost of equity).

Remediation Actions

- If all elements above are satisfied, stay the course and continue with current plans; repeat strategy testing process at least annually.
- If any element fails, initiate analysis to determine whether a new approach, additional actions, or a change to currently expected business results are necessary within anticipated constraints.

Question 3 – Are our plans, which appear to be viable and value creating, actually feasible?

Evidence of a *feasible* strategic plan includes financial and cash flow forecasts which satisfy all conditions of question two above (creating requisite enterprise value) *and:*

- Consist of realistic assumptions and still generate value even under conditions somewhat less favorable than those represented in base assumptions
- Can be achieved within the boundaries our established internal and external financial policies or requirements
- Are based on a sufficient set of available (sustainable or repeatable) opportunities
- Will achieve requisite future value based upon well-understood growth opportunities (such as those that produce predictable revenues or benefits or those within a predicable range of uncertainty)
- Are executable with the current capabilities and capacities of the organization or the plan has properly considered and included the expense of capability and capacity expansion

Question 4 – Is a new approach or change to our existing assumptions, plans, or expectations necessary?

Evidence of the need to question strategy viability and feasibility and consider new options:

- Strategy only delivers requisite value under overly-aggressive or optimistic assumptions.
- Essential factors enumerated in the "working or viable strategy" section above are missing or not satisfied.
- Feasibility is uncertain, or confidence in existing strategies and plans is lacking.
- Assumed opportunity availability has not been demonstrated or validated.

Remediation Actions

- Consider new or different strategic initiatives based on imperatives arising from an examination of the facts which become evident during analysis phase.
- Continue the testing for viability and feasibility (questions two and three) until a demonstrated course of action satisfies all requirements of the "working or viable" and "feasible" sections above.

Question 5 – Does a needed or revised set of initiatives suggest that re-articulation of our core strategy is necessary?

Re-articulation of or additions to the stated strategy may be necessary if:

- Significant new actions are required which change how we should describe the company's future direction and actions.
- The company requires significant changes to capital structure (leveraging, de-leveraging, follow-on stock offering, spin-off, strategic partnerships, and so on).

Remediation Actions

- Articulate, amend, or otherwise modify strategy statements, prioritization, vision, mission, focus, or aspirations as appropriate.
- Socialize changes internally and develop support for and alignment with re-articulation of strategy.
- Make changes public (illustrating rationale) and discuss alignment process.

The first question in the above strategy testing or assessment process can be administered by interviewing at various levels or functions in the organization. It can also be done by means of a survey.

Questions two, three, and four require demonstrating actual numerical analysis, which should be presented to executive leadership. This analysis should also be the topic of survey questions to ensure that *all* members of the leadership team are satisfied and aligned with the facts and assumptions presented. Thus, additional interview questions should include inquiry about the data, analysis, implications, and conclusions.

Question five is about final stages of the alignment process, to ensure you are saying what you are doing and doing what you are saying – so that everyone from the equity markets to the boardroom, conference rooms, and factory floors across the company can be on the same page.

Posing questions to confirm (or call into question) strategy viability can be extremely helpful in demonstrating that you have evidence of a *viable* strategy and plan that you believe creates value. It can be a good indicator of how well and how deeply the strategy is being accepted and internalized by the organization's people.

Chapter 10 – Testing for Strategic Plan Viability
Key Thoughts & Takeaways

Before proceeding to the next chapter, please take a few minutes to think about the following with your organization in mind:

What are my key takeaways from this chapter?

What issues have I observed in my company or organization?

What are the implications for my organization?

11. Conclusions

Pragmatic Strategic Planning Model Leads to More Viable Strategic Plans

With this book, we have attempted to accomplish three things:

1. Provide a pragmatic (doable) model for developing a value-enhancing strategic plan for a business – virtually any type of business

2. Provide guidance and criteria to help insure success *at each stage* of the strategic planning process

3. Provide practical methods to navigate the many barriers to good strategic planning

In pondering the suggestions and processes offered in this guide, we now offer a few *reminders* that contribute to effective strategy development.

Do Your Homework & Gather the Facts

Strategy should not and cannot be developed in a vacuum. It must be based on facts and available data rather than on opinions and personal preferences. Key facts and constraints should reside in the *common fact base* that the executive team relies on to make and support decisions.

Assess & Re-Assess the Relative Strength of Your Business Model

A realistic assessment of the strengths and weaknesses of your firm's business model – and an understanding about where value is migrating today is crucial, not just to the quality of your strategic plan, but to long-term survival of the business.

212

Apply Criteria-Based Decision Making at Each Stage of the Planning Model & Process

It is as important to "decide how we will decide" as it is to actually make decisions. Agreeing first on the criteria for key decisions will increase the quality of and the commitment to the plan. Assumptions should be fully documented and constraints identified.

Work Consistently to Create Alignment around the Plan

Commitment to and alignment around the plan are just as important as the plan itself. Plans that lack commitment and alignment by all key executives are plans that are more likely to fail. Carefully select executive sponsors and Key Initiative leaders in such a way as to create focus and alignment. Develop specific strategies and actions to deal with misalignment issues.

Define Key Strategic Initiatives as the *How* of Your Plan

Choose these initiatives carefully – resource them fully – enable them with good leadership, sponsorship, and metrics for achievement.

Build in Accountability

Set up a process to review and evaluate progress toward accomplishing the key initiatives. Include time deadlines, interim goals, milestones, pilot project completion, internal or external partner assessments, and so on.

Feedback – "Breakfast of Champions"

We welcome your opinions and feedback regarding the use and effectiveness of the methods and approaches we've described. Our desire for the book's content to be truly *pragmatic* is of great importance to our efforts. We will appreciate learning from your experience.

Please direct your comments to:

jhdobbs@pragmaticstrategypartners.com

jfdobbs@pragmaticstrategypartners.com

Appendix A

Rationale for the "Balanced Business Model" Theory

Broadly, a company can focus its efforts toward three desirable outcomes: growth, profitability, and repeatability. Most businesses should be concerned with "profitable operations and profitable growth, repeatedly." Finding a natural speed limit, rhythm, pace, and cadence allows a company to focus on all three broad objectives appropriately and to make efficient use of its resources. For a company to continually create value for its equity holders and its customers, it must operationalize a business model that allows it to at least somewhat balance these objectives.

By way of review, our assertion is that a balanced business model is more likely to reliably create value. To make our case, we must digress briefly to discuss a basic method of determining the value of a company.

A Quick Valuation Method: the "Multiple"

Consider for a moment a commonly used valuation ratio or metric used by Wall Street analysts, the so-called EV/EBITDA "multiple."

Multiple = Enterprise Value / EBITDA

EBITDA is an acronym for "Earnings Before Interest, Taxes, Depreciation, and Amortization." EBITDA is roughly the amount of cash a company is bringing in within a given year after all operating expenses. Enterprise Value is the market value of a company's equity plus the market value of its (net) debt.

The units of this ratio are years : Dollars / (dollars/year) → years. In short, this Wall Street metric says "this company is worth 'X' years of its recent or expected cash flow." Rearranging this ratio gives:

Enterprise Value (\$) = Cash flow (\$/yr) * Multiple (yrs).

If we assume for a moment that this is the appropriate way to value a company, then we can use this equation for a thought exercise. For this exercise, let's assume that the value of the Multiple is 10.

Question: How does a company simply maintain its current value?

Answer: A company maintains its value if:

(1) Both EBITDA expectations and the market Multiple are constant, OR

(2) A change to EBITDA expectations is exactly offset by changes to the multiple:

- EBITDA / (1 + %Change) * Multiple * (1 + %Change) , OR
- EBITDA * (1 + %Change) * Multiple / (1 + %Change)

Any other change to EBITDA expectations, not exactly matched by a change in the multiple, will result in a company value that is higher or lower.

So what causes the multiple to be the value it is? How do we interpret a multiple of "10" in our example? The most common answer to this question is: "That's what the data shows. If we divide the enterprise values of each member the Company's peer group by their corresponding EBITDAs, we see that the answer is 10, on average." While this may be true, it doesn't help us understand why the magnitude of the multiple is what it is, even if we simply observe it to be so. There is a reason why the multiple's magnitude tends to be what it is, and the answer lies in a very fundamental equation of finance.

Finance Primer

The key to understanding the multiple is the concept of a perpetuity. So what is a perpetuity? A perpetuity is a financial instrument in which fixed payments are made at regular, defined intervals, at a specified interest rate "in perpetuity" (i.e., forever). Say you borrowed $10,000, and the lender said to you, "You never have to pay back the principal, you just have to pay me $500 every year forever. The lender would be offering you a loan in the form of a perpetuity. Most of us have no experience with such an instrument, but we generally have experience with something very similar to a perpetuity: a mortgage.

A mortgage is a type of annuity. An annuity is a security in which an equal payment is made in each period for a fixed number of periods at a specified rate of interest. For many of us, a 30-yr mortgage may seem to take forever to pay off, but, after "just 360 monthly payments," the mortgage is paid off. The only difference between an annuity (think mortgage) and a "perpetual annuity" or a "perpetuity" is that in a perpetuity these payments would never end – they would be made "in perpetuity."

Why is this seemingly esoteric concept related to our conversation here? It turns out that the equation relating the valuation of a perpetuity and the periodic payment is shockingly simple. In fact, it is much simpler than the equivalent valuation equation for an annuity. We will avoid the professorial proof and simply present the equation:

Value of a perpetuity = Periodic Payment / (Interest Rate Per Period),

Where interest rate is the "price paid" or "cost" of the capital received up front. Thus, another way to express it would be:

Value of a perpetuity = Periodic Payment / (Cost of Capital Per Period)

Back to the Multiple

Let's juxtapose the perpetuity equation and our multiple valuation equation:

Enterprise Value = Annual EBITDA * Multiple

Perpetuity Value = Periodic Payment / (Cost of Capital Per Period)

An "annual EBITDA," is quite similar to a "periodic payment." Noting this and considering these two equations together we derive an interpretation of the Multiple.

Multiple = 1 / (Cost of Capital)[†]

So, then, the value of a "perpetually operating" firm can be approximated as

$$\text{Enterprise Value (\$) = EBITDA (\$/yr) * 1/(Cost of capital/yr)}$$

If a company's EBITDA is constant and its cost of capital is constant, then our equation suggests that the company's value would be constant. Furthermore, if cost of capital is 10%, then our multiple, which equals 1/Cost of Capital is equal to 10. So if you encounter a valuation by an analyst which suggests that the average peer group multiple is 10, then you can immediately think "that implies the cost of capital for these companies is around 10%."

Repeatability

Let's pause for a minute to think about the implicit implication of this valuation method. We used a perpetuity as a quick valuation for a company. Theoretically, this means that a company would have to produce this EBITDA forever for the enterprise to be worth the value we calculate. So first of all, if the cash flow is expected to be flat, then this represents the absolute maximum the company could be worth, because it is very unlikely that the company would be a going concern forever. So, if a company had a fixed market that could not grow, it would be very important for that company to be able to repeat its performance every single year, which leads us to explore the concept of repeatability or a sustainable business model.

If the company cannot sustain this performance each year, but instead its cash flow declines over time, then each year when the valuation is calculated, it will be worth less than it was a year before. If the company has a sizable existing business but this existing business loses a little ground each year, then the company must replace the losses with new business opportunities just to stay even from a value perspective.

Growth

So what if the cash flow is not expected to be constant? It turns out this is the key to understanding why the multiple would tend to grow or shrink. Again, without proof, it seems that the equation for a "growing perpetuity"

– a perpetuity in which the payments are growing at a fixed rate – is likewise quite straightforward:

Value of Growing Perpetuity = Period Payment (at time zero) /

(InterestRate – GrowthRate)

Stating this in our company valuation form, the equation then becomes:

Enterprise Value ($) = EBITDA ($/yr) *

1/(Cost of capital/yr – GrowthRate/yr)

This is an even more useful equation, because at zero growth it is equivalent to the previous equation, but can be used with positive or negative growth as well. It is also the key to understanding why the multiple may be changing: It has everything to do with growth expectations.

Let's assume that cost of capital is 10% and growth is 0% – the company's cash flow overall is neither growing nor shrinking. Then our multiple is 10 as we have previously stated. But if cash flow is growing overall at a rate of 2%, then the multiple becomes: 1 / (10%-2%) = 1 / 8% = 12.5. So if a company were perceived to be able to sustain a 2% growth forever, its valuation multiple would increase by 25% versus the situation in which the company were perceived to simply maintain its cash flow. That's a shocking difference for a moderate amount of growth! And what leads a company to be perceived to be able to grow like this perpetually? A track record of doing so and a strategic presentation and positioning of its business, illustrating convincingly how it will continue to do this in the future.

With this context, growth is an important component of valuation. This is why companies that are expected to experience significant growth have valuation multiples which are very high. If we take a look at a company like Apple, we find that Apple's EV/EBITDA, at the time of this writing, is 9.4, meaning that the market values the company at less than 10 years of its current EBITDA. It is hard to see how Apple, already the most valuable company in the world, can massively grow its cash flows. In contrast, the same metric (EV/EBITDA) for Facebook is 41! So what kind of growth expectations does this suggest for Facebook? Following the same mathematics demonstrated in the previous paragraph, we would find that Facebook is implicitly expected to grow its cash flows perpetually (forever) at over 7.5%, assuming a cost of capital of 10%. This is a staggering number when you consider that the U.S. economy only grows at 2%-3% per year. Theoretically, if Facebook could do this forever, it would surpass the U.S. economy.

In truth, we know that a company like Facebook is not going to grow its cash flows at a nice steady rate forever, especially not at a rate more than twice that of the economy as a whole. What it will do is grow very substantially in the near term – say, 25% per year over the next 5 years – and then its growth will slow – say, 2% by year 10. At that point, Facebook's multiple would be in line with that of the S&P 500. This is exactly what is represented by its very sizeable multiple.

So one question that might be asked is: How many years effectively does a company have to produce cash flows to justify its valuation? The perpetuity equation is founded upon the principles of present value and future value. In fact, the perpetuity equation would state that if I receive $100 each year in perpetuity, the present value of those cash flows gets smaller and smaller the further out into the future one considers. If we go with our multiple of 10 – equivalent to our cost of capital, discount rate, or interest rate of 10% – then we find the following:

1st 5 years of cash flow represent approximately 41% of the perpetuity's value

1st 7 years: 52%

1st 10 years: 65%

1st 15 years: 79%

1st 20 years: 88%

1st 22 years: 90%

1st 28 years: 95%

Clearly the majority of a company's value – even for a firm that is expected to only maintain flat levels of cash flows – is dependent upon a period of time we can wrap our minds around. To get to a simple majority of over 50% of value requires a mere 7 years.

Putting It All together

Here is a sobering thought: Regardless of whether or not a company is growing, it takes many years of cash flow generation to justify the valuation of a company. And when Wall Street analysts are valuing a company, they need to be able to see and understand where these future cash flows are going to come from. If analysts perceive that next year's cash flows are going to be anemic compared to this year, then even if they were to apply the same multiple to that single year cash flow, the enterprise value they compute will be lower than what they would have computed for this year. This is not the end of the world if they can see that this will turn around and be stronger in subsequent years, but if they can't see this, then the result will be a lower valuation. To confirm a company's current valuation, certainly to justify a higher valuation, analysts need to be able to see or perceive/believe that future cash flows will be equal to or greater than what they are now. They need to anticipate "repeatability" in what the company has just delivered. A multiple valuation is simple to compute and is thus widely used as a metric; however, if it turns out that revenues or growth proved to be not quite as strong as originally thought, it can quickly lead to an overvalued company and subsequent decline in the price of its stock.

So the valuation of a company in simple terms comes down to three things:

- **Profitability** – positive EBITDA or excess cash flows after all operating expenses, and ultimately, positive cash flow after all investment, interest, and taxes

- **Growth** – the extent to which a company's cash flows are expected to change over time
- **Repeatability** – sustainably renewing its portfolio of opportunities year after year in order to maintain its ability to generate cash flows well into the future

This is the theoretical basis behind the importance of keeping all three objectives of a balanced business model in mind at all times. Too narrow a focus on one area over time will invariably lead to problems in one (or both) of the other areas. Growth at all costs will erode profitability and make repeatability suspect, leading to lagging valuations later. A singular focus on profitability will detract from the real efforts required to ensure that the business can continue doing what it must do well into the future and may detract from growing new opportunities that are necessary even in order to maintain cash flows.

Notes and References

Chapter 1

1. Darrell Rigby and Barbara Bilodeau, *Management Tools and Trends 2015*, Bain & Company.

2. A.T. Kearney, "Strategy Survey," 2014.

3. G. C. Kane, D. Palmer, A. N. Phillips, D. Kiron, and N. Buckley, "Strategy, not Technology Drives Digital Transformation," *MIT Sloan Management Review and Deloitte University Press,* July 2015.

4. Herminia Ibarra, "The Way to Become a Strategic Executive," *The Wall Street Journal,* February 23, 2015.

5. Jacques Bughin, Laura LaBerge, and Anette Mellbye, "The Case for Digital Reinvention," *McKinsey Quarterly,* February 2017.

6. Natasha Khan, "Beijing Puts Robots to Work," *The Wall Street Journal,* August 27, 2018.

7. "How to Improve Strategic Planning," *McKinsey Quarterly,* August 2007.

8. Mark Judah, Dunnigan O"Keefe, David Zehner and Lucy Cummings, "Strategic Planning That Produces Real Strategy," Bain & Company, www.bain.com February 10, 2016.

9. Henry Mintzberg, "Crafting Strategy," *Harvard Business Review,* July 1987.

10. "Rethinking the Role of the Strategist," *McKinsey Quarterly,* November 2014.

11. Herminia Ibarra, "The Way to Become a Strategic Executive," *The Wall Street Journal,* February 23, 2015.

Chapter 3

1. Jeffrey Pfeffer and Robert I. Sutton, "Evidence-Based Management," *Harvard Business Review,* January 2006.

2. Hugh Courtney, Jane Kirkland, and S. Patrick Viguerie, "Strategy Under Uncertainty," *McKinsey Quarterly* June 2000.

3. PwC, 18th Annual CEO Survey, Full Report http://www.pwc.com/us/en/ceosurvey/index.html?WT.mc_id =cs_us-hero-home_CEO-survey.

4. "New PwC Survey: CEOs Embrace Digital Transformation," *Forbes.com* (technology) February 27, 2015.

5. Arne Gast and Paul Lansink, "Digital hives: Creating a surge around change," *McKinsey Quarterly* April 2015.

Chapter 4

1. Barry Sheehy, Hyler Bracey, and Rick Frazier, *Winning the Race for Value: Strategies to Create Competitive Advantage* (Amacom Press, 1996).

2. John H. Dobbs, "Competition's New Battleground: The Integrated Value Chain," Cambridge Technology Partners White Paper, 1998.

3. Jack Ma, "America's Online Sales Opportunity in China," *The Wall Street Journal,* June 9, 2015.

4. Heather Brilliant and Elizabeth Collins, Why Moats Matter: The Morningstar Approach to Stock Investing (Morningstar).

5. Ram Charan, The Attacker's Advantage: Turning Uncertainty Into Breakthrough Opportunities (Perseus Book Group, 2015).

6. "Better to be the Disruptor than the Disrupted," *The Wall Street Journal,* February 23, 2015.

7. Leigh Buchanan, "Building a Better Model," *Inc. Magazine* December 2014.

8. Brad Stone, "A Virtual Garage Sale Takes on Craigslist," *Bloomberg Business Week* (Technology), April 6-12, 2015.

9. Arandjelovic, Bulin, and Khan, "Why CIOs Should Be Business Strategy Partners," *McKinsey Quarterly* February 2015.

10. Kim S. Nash, "Instant Innovation," *CIO Magazine,* February 15, 2015.

11. Martha Heller, "Reaching the Next Horizon," *CIO Magazine,* March 1, 2015.

12. Kim S. Nash, "Corporate Boards Turn Focus to Tech Strategy, Weaknesses," *The Wall Street Journal,* April 7, 2015.

13. Joann S. Lublin, "The Newest Board Member: Digital," *The Wall Street Journal,* June 10, 2015.

14. Salim Ismail, "Exponential Organizations: Why new organizations are ten times better, faster, and cheaper than yours (and what to do about it)," *The Wall Street Journal – CIO Journal,* June 11, 2015.

15. Thornton A. May, "Things IT leaders need to be thinking about to prepare for what's coming," *Computerworld,* June 11, 2015.

16. Douglas MacMillan, "The $50 Billion Question: Can Uber Deliver?," *The Wall Street Journal,* June 16, 2015.

17. Steven A. Cohen and Matthew W Granade, "Models Will Run the World," *The Wall Street Journal,* August 20, 2018.

18. Marc de Jong and Menno van Dijk, "Disrupting beliefs: A new approach to business-model innovation," *McKinsey Quarterly,* July 2015.

19. Christina Rogers, "GM, Ford Flourish Out of the Limelight," *The Wall Street Journal,* July 29, 2015.

20. Yoko Kubota, "Subaru Maker's Profit Margin Outpaces Larger Rivals," *The Wall Street Journal,* August 1, 2015.

Chapter 5

1. Isaiah 28:7.
2. www.google.com.
3. "Start-up Cities: The Best Places to Start a New Business in America," *PM* February 2015.
4. www.WellstarHealth.org.
5. www.amazon.com.
6. www.generalelectric.com.
7. www.merck.com.
8. Sir Martin Sorrell, "China a Threat? Some Take Risks Like Jack Ma," *The Telegraph,* April 11, 2015.
9. www.CureAlzheimers.org.
10. G. C. Kane, D. Palmer, A. N. Phillips, D. Kiron, and N. Buckley, "Strategy, not Technology Drives Digital Transformation," *MIT Sloan Management Review and Deloitte University Press,* July 2015.
11. "A Coach's View of Leadership: Lou Holtz on what holds a business together," *The Wall Street Journal Report CEO Council,* November 24, 2015.

Chapter 6

1. "Cook on Apple's Corporate Culture: World's 50 Best Leaders", *Fortune Magazine,* April 1, 2015.

2. Geoff Colvin, "Personal Bests: The 100 Best Companies to Work For," *Fortune Magazine,* March 15, 2015.
3. Google – Corporate Web Site.
4. Boeing – Corporate Web Site.
5. UPS – Corporate Web Site.
6. "A Coach's View of Leadership: Lou Holtz on what holds a business together," *The Wall Street Journal Report CEO Council,* November 24, 2015.

Chapter 7

1. A.T. Kearney, "Strategy Survey," 2014.
2. Martin Hirt and Paul Willmott, "Strategic Principles for competing in the digital age," *McKinsey Quarterly,* May 2014.
3. "Everyone's Catching a Ride on the Delivery-app Bandwagon," *INC. Magazine,* February 2015.
4. "Car Crisis? Help is on the Way," *CIO Magazine,* January 1, 2015.
5. Barry Sheehy, Hyler Bracey, & Rick Frazier, *Winning the Race for Value: Strategies to Create Competitive Advantage* (Amacom Press, 1996).

Chapter 8

1. "Leadership Lessons from the Generals," *The Wall Street Journal,* December 9, 2014.
2. Louis V. Gerstner Jr., "Can Strategic Planning Pay Off?" *McKinsey Quarterly,* December 1973.
3. "UPS Unveils Plans to Improve Delivery Performance," *The Wall Street Journal,* January 30, 2014.

4. "UPS, FedEx Gird for an Earlier Holiday Rush," *The Wall Street Journal,* November 18, 2014.

5. "No Gift? Blame Santa, not UPS," *Atlanta Journal-Constitution,* December 25, 2014.

6. "One Day, 34 Million Packages at UPS," *The Wall Street Journal,* December 22, 2014.

7. "Health Site's Setup Slammed," *The Wall Street Journal,* January 21, 2015.

8. "Creative Destruction at a Broker Near You," *The Wall Street Journal,* May 5, 2015.

9. *Atlanta Journal,* February 3, 2016.

Chapter 9

1. "Enduring Ideas: Portfolio of Initiatives," *McKinsey Quarterly,* October 2009.

About the Authors

John H. Dobbs is an experienced consultant in the areas of Strategic Planning, Business Process Redesign, Information Technology & Business Integration Strategies and Organization Change Management. He has consulted on business and process strategy, IT and internet strategy issues with a variety of clients including: Johnson & Johnson; United Parcel Service; Coca-Cola; BB&T; SE Toyota Distributors; CNN; Nationwide Insurance; State of Ohio; Honda of America; Hospital Corp of America (HCA); Tenet Healthcare; Royal Caribbean; and others. He is a graduate of The University of Utah and as well holds an MBA degree from the University of Pittsburgh. He has been employed by Johnson & Johnson, DDI; The Atlanta Consulting Group; Cambridge Technology Partners; Novell and Cisco Systems. He currently resides in Marietta, GA.

John F. Dobbs is an experienced corporate strategic planning and finance professional, most recently serving as Vice President of Strategy, Planning, and Performance Management at Murphy USA, a fuel and convenience retailer ranked 175th on the Fortune 500 in 2014. He began his career as a petroleum engineer at ExxonMobil, and from there joined Ryder Scott Company as a specialized technical consultant for clients including Pemex, PDVSA, ENI, Chevron, Repsol, among others. After earning his MBA in Finance at Tulane University, John moved into business development and strategic planning roles starting with a position as financial analyst in the strategy group for Hess Corporation. He then joined Murphy Oil Corporation, serving in various positions including Corporate Reserves Manager, Business Development Manager, and General Manager Corporate Planning. In 2013, Murphy Oil spun off its U.S. retail fuel business into an independent publicly traded company, Murphy USA. John holds a B.S. in Chemical Engineering from BYU and currently resides in Houston, TX.

Printed in Great Britain
by Amazon

18719158R00136